Cyber Certainty

Threat Reduction for Business Leaders

CYBER CERTAINTY

THREAT REDUCTION FOR BUSINESS LEADERS

DANIEL TOBOK

Print ISBN: 978-1-7382942-3-7
Ebook ISBN 978-1-7382942-4-4

10 9 8 7 6 5 4 3 2 1

Disclaimer: Every possible effort has been made to ensure that the information contained in this book is accurate at the time of going to press, and the publisher and author cannot accept responsibility for any errors or omissions, however caused. No responsibility for loss or damage occasioned to any person acting, or refraining from action, as a result of the material in this publication can be accepted by the editor, the publisher or any of the authors.

Edited by: Don Loney
Interior Design by Kevin R Coleman
Cover Art by Biserka Design

515 Madison Avenue
Suite 8192
New York, New York 10022

Contents

INTRODUCTION

NO ORGANIZATION IS IMMUNE FROM CYBER CRIME

When large institutions are the victim of a cyberattack, media coverage ensues and people get a snapshot of the nature of the attack, the possible perpetrators, and the victims. But snapshots fall terribly short of communicating the rest of the story. For businesses that are not paying attention—and there appears to be no shortage of them—the consequences of being hacked, having files held for ransom, and intellectual property stolen can be a very expensive, and unnecessary, learning experience.

In a recent report published in *USA Today*, the scope of cyber threats is frightening:

> "It's hard to know exactly how many cyberattacks occur daily as not all are reported. It's estimated that one occurs every 39 seconds, but businesses were expected to be attacked every 11 seconds in 2021.[1] According to Cybersecurity Ventures, the cost of damage caused by cyberattacks globally is around $16.4 billion a day — or $190,000 a second.[2]
>
> It is estimated that attacks on businesses, consumers, governments and devices will happen every two seconds by 2023.[3] According to Sectigo, around 4.1 million websites were being affected by malware worldwide in 2022.[4] The report also stated that 48% of small business owners think their websites are too small to be a target.
>
> Since the FBI set up the IC3 in 2000 to receive cybercrime-related complaints, it has received an average of 651,800 per year.[5]"

Fending off cyber threats is known as the domain of cybersecurity. When cybersecurity for whatever reasons fails to protect the organization, the organization ends up responding to threats and breaches after they have occurred. Crisis management protocols guide next steps and a post-mortem invariably recommends stronger cybersecurity measures be put in place. In the meantime, the organization suffers damage to its reputation and loss of IP, and people lose their personal data to cyber criminals. For these reasons, this book takes a different approach to getting out in front of cyber threats. It is a shift from reactive cybersecurity to a proactive and holistic framework known as Cyber Certainty.

Cyber Certainty is more than a strategy; it is a mindset that integrates awareness, preparedness, literacy and resilience into the core of organizational culture. At its essence, Cyber Certainty addresses our fundamental human concern for security and certainty in an increasingly uncertain digital landscape. This posture extends beyond merely defending against cyber threats; it encompasses understanding and managing our relationship with these threats in a proactive, informed and resilient manner.

The cornerstone of Cyber Certainty is the Cyber Quotient—a comprehensive metric that evaluates an organization's or business' vulnerability in the face of cyber threats. This metric goes beyond technical assessments, incorporating elements of cyber consciousness, preparedness, literacy, and response. Organizations that use the Cyber Quotient can assess its systems and responses in regard to withstanding and recovering from cyber incidents.

This book is designed to guide business leaders, IT professionals and cybersecurity enthusiasts through the intricate journey of achieving Cyber Certainty It articulates the complexities of modern cyber threats, the evolving role of the C-suite in cybersecurity and the accountability of small business owners, and the strategies required to build a cyber-resilient organization. Through real-world case studies, practical advice, and forward-thinking strategies, the book aims to equip the reader with the knowledge and tools necessary to navigate the digital future with confidence and certainty. Welcome to a new era of cybersecurity—welcome to Cyber Certainty.

ENDNOTES

1 Medhi Punjawi and Sierra Campbell, "Cybersecurity statistics in 2024," USA Today (March 27, 2024), Cybersecurity Ventures – Global Ransomware Damage Costs Predicted to Reach $20 Billion (USD) by 2021.

2 Punjawi and Campbell, USA Today (March 27, 2024), Cybersecurity Ventures – Cybercrime to Cost the World $10.5 Trillion Annually by 2025.

3 Punjawi and Campbell, USA Today (March 27, 2024), Cybersecurity Ventures – Top 10 Cybersecurity Predictions and Statistics for 2024.

4 Punjawi and Campbell, USA Today (March 27, 2024), Sectigo's Research Finds Websites Attacked 172 Times a Day & Automated Bot Attacks on the Rise for SMBs.

5 Punjawi and Campbell, USA Today (March 27, 2024), Federal Bureau of Investigation – Internet Crime Complaint Center 2022 Statistics.

A Message From the Author

Dear Business Leader:

In today's rapidly evolving digital landscape, the importance of cybersecurity cannot be overstated. As the CEO of CYPFER, I've witnessed firsthand the challenges businesses face in navigating the complexities of digital defense. It's not just about technology; it's about understanding the broader implications of our interconnected world.

I wrote this guide to demystify the world of cybersecurity for business owners like you. This book is a culmination of over two decades of experience-driven results, insights and lessons learned in the trenches of cyber restoration and defense. It's not just a guide—it's a testament to the resilience and innovation that defines our industry. My hope is that, as you turn each page, you'll gain a deeper understanding of the cyber challenges you face and the tools at your disposal.

More than that, I want you to feel empowered. Cybersecurity isn't a destination—it's a journey. And with the right knowledge and mindset, it's a journey you can undertake with confidence. Remember, in the realm of cybersecurity, knowledge is your greatest ally. Equip yourself with it, stay vigilant and always be ready to adapt. I believe that with the insights from this book, you'll be well on your way to achieving true cyber certainty. I wish you a secure and prosperous digital future.

Daniel Tobok
CEO, CYPFER

CHAPTER 1

THE DIGITAL LANDSCAPE: OPPORTUNITY AND THREAT

The digital age has ushered in an era of unprecedented change, fundamentally reshaping the way we communicate, conduct business and interact with the world around us. To understand the role of cybersecurity today, and in the future, it is necessary to provide an overview of the current digital landscape and lay the groundwork for the comprehensive discussions that will follow on the implications, challenges and strategies within this transformative era.

The rise of the internet in the late 20th century marked the onset of what would become a global digital transformation. This transformation has accelerated with advancements in technology, particularly with the proliferation of the internet, mobile technology and, more recently, the Internet of Things (IoT). We live in a hyper-connected world where billions of devices are interconnected, communicating continuously and creating vast networks that span the globe. These networks facilitate a continuous flow of information, driving efficiencies in industries as diverse as healthcare, finance, education and manufacturing. However, the benefits of this digital interconnectedness come with their own set of challenges.

One of the most pressing challenges in today's digital landscape is the management and security of the vast volumes of data generated every second. Every interaction, transaction and digital activity generates data, contributing to an ever-expanding digital footprint. This data is an invaluable asset for organizations, but also poses significant risks if not managed and secured properly. Data breaches have become increasingly common and are now a significant threat to organizations of all sizes. These breaches occur when unauthorized parties gain access to sensitive data, often leading to financial loss, reputational damage and legal consequences. The frequency and sophistication of these attacks highlight the critical need for robust cybersecurity measures.

Challenges in the Digital Landscape

As the digital world continues to expand, it introduces myriad challenges that must be navigated with caution and strategic foresight. The very fabric of our digital existence is punctuated with issues ranging from security vulnerabilities to privacy concerns, each presenting unique hurdles for individuals, organizations, and societies at large.

1. Security Vulnerabilities

One of the most pressing challenges in today's digital landscape is the escalating threat of cybersecurity vulnerabilities. As we connect more devices to the internet from smartphones and laptops to home appliances and vehicles, each becomes a potential vector for cyberattacks. The complexity and interconnectedness of these systems often amplify the potential impacts of such breaches, making them not only more common but also more damaging.

Cyber threats have evolved in sophistication, moving from isolated incidents of malware to coordinated attacks against critical infrastructure. These incidents can disrupt services, steal sensitive data and even bring daily functioning of a society to a halt. Organizations face the continuous task of updating their cybersecurity protocols to ward off these threats, a process that requires constant vigilance and significant investment. Cybersecurity is no longer a niche concern of IT departments but a foundational business consideration that impacts every level of an organization. The challenge is not only in implementing effective security measures, but also in maintaining them against an ever-evolving threat landscape.

2. Data Overload

The digital age is marked by an unprecedented explosion of data, commonly referred to as "big data." This surge is driven by the proliferation of digital devices and sensors, as well as by an increase in online activities. While data can be an invaluable asset for businesses offering insights into customer behavior, operational efficiency and emerging market trends, the volume and sensitivity of data also present significant challenges in terms of management and security. Organizations must develop data management systems to handle, store and analyze the vast amounts of information. Moreover, they need robust data security measures to protect this information from breaches, which could have devastating financial and reputational consequences.

The challenge extends beyond mere technological solutions; it requires a holistic approach that includes legal, regulatory and ethical considerations, especially in industries handling sensitive information.

3. Privacy Concerns

As digital platforms become more integrated into our personal and professional lives, they increasingly influence our privacy. The convenience of digital solutions comes at the cost of exposing more of our personal information to potential misuse. High-profile data breaches have exposed the vulnerabilities in systems supposedly designed to protect personal information, leading to increased public and regulatory scrutiny. Privacy concerns are not just about unauthorized access to data; they also encompass how data is used by those who collect it. This has led to calls for greater transparency and control for users over their own data, as well as stricter regulations like the General Data Protection Regulation (GDPR) in the European Union. Organizations must navigate these regulations while still leveraging data to offer better and more personalized services.

4. The Digital Divide

Despite the widespread adoption of digital technology, a significant divide remains between those who have full access to digital tools and those who do not. This digital divide is often delineated along lines of geography, income and education, with profound implications for social equity and economic opportunity. Bridging this divide is crucial for ensuring that the benefits of the digital revolution are shared equitably across all sectors of society.

Efforts to address the digital divide must focus on both access and education. Providing infrastructure and connectivity are only part of the solution; equipping people with the necessary skills to utilize digital technologies effectively is equally important. This challenge requires concerted efforts from governments, private organizations and civil society to create inclusive digital policies that empower all individuals. Navigating these challenges requires a multifaceted approach that balances technological innovation with ethical considerations, regulatory compliance and social inclusivity. As we progress even further into the digital era, the solutions to these challenges will shape the future of our digital landscape, influencing how we live, work and interact with the world around us.

Opportunities in the Digital Landscape

While the digital landscape is fraught with challenges, each challenge also presents an opportunity for improvement and innovation. For instance, the security vulnerabilities that led to breaches like that at Equifax (discussed later in this chapter) also catalyze advancements in cybersecurity technologies and practices. Similarly, while the data overload presents significant challenges in data management, it also drives innovation in data analysis and storage solutions, such as advancements in big data technology and cloud computing.

Opportunities for innovation, economic growth and improved efficiency across various sectors are reshaping industries, transforming consumer interactions and redefining the very nature of competition and cooperation on a global scale.

1. Innovation and Economic Growth

Digital technologies serve as a powerful catalyst for innovation and economic development. They provide businesses with tools to create new models and services that disrupt traditional markets and establish new norms. For example, e-commerce platforms like Amazon and Alibaba have revolutionized retail by offering unprecedented convenience, variety and accessibility to consumers worldwide. Similarly, fintech companies use technology to provide innovative financial services that are faster, more accessible, and often cheaper than traditional banking services. These innovations not only stimulate economic growth by creating new markets and jobs, but also drive efficiency across sectors.

Digital tools enable businesses to streamline operations, reduce costs and enhance productivity. Cloud computing, for instance, allows businesses to scale rapidly without the need for significant capital investments in physical infrastructure. Moreover, the digital economy is increasingly democratized, allowing small startups to compete with large corporations through innovation and agility.

2. Enhanced Connectivity

The digital age has brought about a revolution in connectivity, making it possible to communicate with anyone, anywhere, at any time. This enhanced connectivity has transformed personal relationships by maintaining connections over long distances more easily than ever before. Social media platforms like Facebook, Instagram and Twitter connect people across the globe, allowing for the sharing of ideas and experiences in real-time. In the business world, digital connectivity has facilitated global operations and collaborations that were previously impossible or prohibitively expensive. Companies can now operate in multiple countries more efficiently, managing international supply chains and reaching global markets with relative ease. This connectivity fosters an integrated world economy, where businesses must consider global impacts and opportunities in their strategies.

3. Improved Decision-Making

The advent of big data and advanced analytical tools has transformed decision-making processes in organizations. With vast amounts of data at their disposal, companies can leverage analytics to gain deep insights into customer behavior, market trends and operational efficiency. Tools like predictive analytics and machine learning algorithms enable businesses to forecast future trends and make proactive decisions. For instance, retailers use big data to optimize their inventory based on predictive models of consumer behavior, thereby minimizing waste and maximizing sales. In healthcare, data analysis helps in predicting outbreaks, understanding patient outcomes and personalizing treatments, which significantly improves the quality of care.

Moreover, artificial intelligence (AI) is becoming integral in processing and making sense of the massive data generated daily. AI systems can identify patterns and insights at a speed and accuracy that humans cannot match, leading to more informed and timely decisions. This capability is particularly crucial in industries where real-time decision-making can mean the difference between profit and loss, such as in finance and manufacturing.

The opportunities presented by the digital landscape are profound and far-reaching. They offer the potential not only for economic growth and operational efficiency but also for significant social benefits, such as improved access to information, education and healthcare. As digital technologies continue to evolve, they will undoubtedly unveil new opportunities that we can scarcely imagine today. However, leveraging these opportunities will require continuous innovation, adaptability and a commitment to addressing the accompanying challenges, particularly those related to security, privacy and inequality.

The Equifax Data Breach

In September 2017, Equifax, one of the largest credit reporting agencies in the United States, disclosed a massive data breach that had exposed the personal information of approximately 148 million people.[1] This breach, resulting from a failure to patch a known vulnerability in the Apache Struts framework, compromised sensitive personal information and had far-reaching implications for the company's reputation and financial stability. It underscored the devastating impact of cybersecurity vulnerabilities and sparked a global conversation about the responsibilities of corporations to protect consumer data.

The vulnerability in question had been identified and a patch issued months before the breach occurred. However, delays in applying the patch—a fundamental and routine aspect of cybersecurity maintenance—led to a window of opportunity for cybercriminals. They exploited this oversight to access vast amounts of sensitive personal data, including Social Security numbers, birthdates, business and home addresses and, in some instances, driver's license numbers.

The fallout from this breach was profound. It affected millions of consumers, compromising their personal and financial information and exposing them to identity theft and fraud. For Equifax, the breach resulted in significant financial losses, including a direct hit to its market valuation, and substantial legal and regulatory repercussions. The company faced lawsuits from affected consumers and investigations by government bodies, which scrutinized Equifax's cybersecurity practices and crisis management response.

No Organization Is Immune

The Equifax incident highlighted critical vulnerabilities not only within one company but also within the cybersecurity strategies employed by many organizations. It served as a wake-up call to the industry about the dangers of complacency and the importance of adhering to best practices in cybersecurity. The breach underscored the necessity for timely updates, vigilant security monitoring and comprehensive risk management strategies.

The breach also had legislative and regulatory implications, sparking debates about the need for stricter data protection laws and improved oversight of cybersecurity practices across industries. It emphasized the broader implications of cybersecurity failures in a world increasingly driven by data and digital transactions.

The lessons from the Equifax breach serve as a stark reminder of the vulnerabilities inherent in digital systems. First, the necessity of maintaining rigorous cybersecurity measures cannot be overstated. Organizations must ensure that all systems are regularly updated and patches applied promptly to mitigate vulnerabilities. Second, proactive threat detection is paramount. Organizations must invest in advanced security technologies and practices that can detect and counter threats before they lead to a breach. Additionally, the Equifax breach demonstrated the need for swift action in addressing known vulnerabilities. Delayed responses can have disastrous consequences, not just for the directly affected organization but also for millions of individuals whose data may be compromised.

The Equifax breach serves as a cautionary tale and a call to action, emphasizing the need for vigilant, proactive and dynamic cybersecurity strategies in the face of a digital landscape that is growing more integrated and complex. The challenge for businesses and regulators is to balance the undeniable benefits of digital innovation with the risks associated with these advancements, particularly concerning security and privacy. To navigate this terrain successfully, organizations must build cybersecurity into their culture and invest in ongoing education for their employees. These steps are essential not only for protecting the organization and its assets against threats, but also for rebuilding trust with consumers and partners—trust which can be so easily damaged.

To that end, what befell Equifax sets the stage for a deeper exploration of the role that leadership plays in an organization's cybersecurity posture. In chapter two we will discuss the responsibilities of the executive leadership team in not only acting to prevent such breaches, but also in fostering a culture of cyber resilience. Leadership must prioritize putting into place cybersecurity strategies that are integrated with core operations, align with organizational goals, and face the broader challenges of the digital age.

ENDNOTES

1. "Equifax Data Breach Settlement," Federal Trade Commission, EPIC - Equifax Data Breach, https://www.ftc.gov/enforcement/refunds/equifax-data-breach-settlement

Chapter 2

The Executive Team's Role in Cybersecurity Initiatives

The rapid advancement of digital technologies has brought cybersecurity to the forefront of leadership oversight. Leadership defines how capable an organization is in defending against cyber threats. The executive team's role has evolved from oversight to active engagement, wherein the strategic direction is set for arming the organization against cyber crime.

Historically, cybersecurity has been viewed as a technical issue delegated to IT professionals. However, as cyber threats have grown in scale and sophistication, impacting critical national infrastructures, financial systems and the private information of billions of consumers, it has become clear that cybersecurity is a strategic business issue. High-profile breaches have shown that the consequences of cybersecurity failures can devastate a company's finances, tarnish its reputation and jeopardize its survival.

Therefore, the business leaderes have a duty to understand the technical foundations of cybersecurity and integrate this knowledge into the broader business risk framework. This integration enables informed decision-making that balances risk with opportunity and aligns with the overall strategic objectives of the organization. Cybersecurity is no longer about threat prevention, but rather managing risk in a way that allows the company to operate and innovate securely.

Shaping a Cybersecurity Culture

Business leaders play a crucial role in shaping a cybersecurity culture. Their commitment to understanding and managing cyber risks sets the tone for prioritization at every level of the organization. When leaders demonstrate that cybersecurity is a priority by investing in the right tools, technologies and talent, they send a powerful message throughout the organization. This top-down emphasis on the importance of security will cultivate a culture where every employee feels responsible for cybersecurity.

Furthermore, in an interconnected world, where businesses operate in a complex ecosystem of digital technologies and third-party services, an executive's accountability extends beyond internal operations. They must also oversee their organization's external cybersecurity practices, ensuring that partners and vendors adhere to the same stringent standards. This holistic approach to cybersecurity governance requires that executives remain continuously informed about the latest threats and trends in the cybersecurity space. The need for knowledgeable, proactive leadership has never been greater. This chapter details the responsibilities of senior executives in cybersecurity, from setting the vision and allocating resources to leading by example and building strong external partnerships. Leaders who do this are not just at the helm of their organization; they are at the forefront of securing the future of our digital world.

Setting and Implementing the Vision

Strategic leadership in cybersecurity begins with the executie team's ability to set a clear and compelling vision—one that articulates the security measures the organization will implement and how such measures integrate into the broader business objectives. An effective cybersecurity vision serves as a guiding light for the organization, informing decision-making at all levels and across all departments.[1]

The first step in setting a vision for cybersecurity involves recognizing it as integral to the organization's overall health and success. In other words, it is both vision and business strategy. This recognition shifts cybersecurity from being viewed merely as a series of technical challenges to being a cornerstone of enterprise risk management. For example, a leader must see cybersecurity as not just about defending against threats but as an enabler of digital transformation and an enhancer of business value. Thus the measures are dynamic and adaptable.

A comprehensive cybersecurity vision should align with the organization's broader strategic goals. This alignment ensures that cybersecurity measures support business objectives rather than hinder them. For instance, if a company aims to expand its digital services, the cybersecurity vision should include resilient measures to protect new digital platforms, thus supporting the company's growth rather than imposing unnecessary restrictions.

To develop this vision, executives should collaborate closely with cybersecurity experts and IT leaders within their organizations. This collaboration can help ensure that the vision is informed by a deep understanding of the cyber risks specific to their industry and technology landscape. The vision should be forward-looking and anticipate cybersecurity challenges and the evolving nature of threats.

Once the vision is established, it must be communicated across the organization. This communication is not just about sending emails or making speeches; it involves integrating the cybersecurity vision into all aspects of business operations. It requires executives to lead by example, demonstrating their commitment to the vision through their actions and decisions.

For example, when a company decides to adopt new cloud technologies, leaders should actively discuss how these technologies align with the company's cybersecurity vision. They should be involved in reviewing and approving security protocols that accompany the adoption of new technologies, thus reinforcing the importance of security in the company's strategic decisions.

Finally, the cybersecurity vision should be embedded into the corporate culture. This embedding can be achieved through training staff, articulating cybersecurity as a corporate value, and by making security a part of the criteria for evaluating the performance of all employees, not just the IT department. By embedding cybersecurity into the corporate culture, executives ensure that it becomes a shared responsibility, with every employee becoming a custodian of the organization's digital safety.

IBM's Cybersecurity Strategy

A prime example of successful integration of cybersecurity into a company's core mission is seen in the approach taken by IBM. Under the leadership of its former CEO Ginni Rometty, IBM reshaped its strategy to prioritize cybersecurity, recognizing it as foundational to the company's overall mission. IBM not only invested heavily in cybersecurity technologies but also launched enterprise-level initiatives like the IBM Security Command

Center, which serves as an innovation hub for developing new security solutions.[2] This proactive approach helped solidify IBM's reputation as a leader in digital security and demonstrated how C-suite leadership can drive a security-first culture.

Allocating Resources

The allocation of resources to cybersecurity is another critical area where leaders play a vital role. Investing in top-tier security technologies and recruiting the best talent are necessary steps in fortifying an organization's defenses. However, determining the right amount to invest in cybersecurity can be challenging. Leaders must balance the need to protect the organization with the need to invest in other areas of the business.

An effective method for budgeting in cybersecurity involves benchmarking against industry standards and assessing the potential cost of security breaches. For instance, financial institutions, due to the high-risk nature of their data, typically allocate a larger percentage of their IT budget to cybersecurity compared to other industries. Following a risk assessment, a company might decide that the potential cost of a data breach justifies a significant investment in cybersecurity, thus aligning the budget with the organization's risk appetite and compliance requirements.

Leading by Example

Executives can have a profound impact on the organizational culture regarding cybersecurity. By leading by example, they can foster a security-first mindset throughout the company. This leadership is crucial in demonstrating to employees at all levels that cybersecurity is a serious priority for the organization.

Effective leadership practices in cybersecurity include regular participation in security training alongside employees, adherence to the same security protocols expected of their teams, and public recognition of good security practices. For example, when executives openly commend departments or individuals who excel in maintaining security standards, it reinforces the importance of everyone's role in safeguarding the company's assets.

To effectively lead in cybersecurity, executives must stay informed about the latest threats, trends and innovations. Engaging with cybersecurity experts through conferences and webinars, specialized training and reviewing current industry literature is essential. A notable example is the CEO of a major healthcare provider who participated in cybersecurity simulations. These exercises served to broaden the CEO's understanding of the potential threats as well as showcasing to the entire organization the executive's direct involvement in and commitment to cybersecurity.

Strengthening cybersecurity also means engaging with external partners. A case in point involves a technology firm that collaborated with law-enforcement agencies and other corporations in joint cybersecurity initiatives. These partnerships facilitated shared insights on emerging threats and best practices, greatly enhancing the firm's security measures.

By setting a good example, staying informed and fostering collaborative relationships, executives play a necessary role in guiding strategic and operational efforts to protect valuable data and systems in an increasingly complex digital landscape.[3]

Anticipating Future Challenges

Business leaders must remain vigilant about the ever-changing nature of cybersecurity threats, among them ransomeware, deep fakes and AI-powered threats, which through their sophistication are capable of bypassing traditional security measures. Additionally, the expanding Internet of Things (IoT) ecosystem, with billions of connected devices, introduces vast attack surfaces that could be exploited to cause unprecedented disruption.

To prepare for these challenges, leaders must adopt a proactive approach. This involves:

- keeping abreast of the latest developments in cybersecurity;

- fostering a culture of continuous learning and adaptation within the organization;

- implementing regular security audits and risk assessments; and

- updating crisis management protocols.

Leaders must also ensure that their organizations adopt a zero-trust security model, which assumes breach and verifies each request as though it originates from an open network.

Preparation includes investing in training and development programs to equip employees with the skills necessary to recognize and respond to cyber threats effectively. Since human error remains one of the largest vulnerabilities in cybersecurity, continuous employee education on the latest phishing tactics and other cyber threats is essential.

Moreover, executives should advocate for and implement a more integrated approach to cybersecurity. This means aligning cybersecurity strategies closely with business objectives, thereby ensuring that security considerations are woven into the fabric of business decision-making processes.

Integrating cybersecurity with business strategy enhances the resilience of the organization and helps in leveraging cybersecurity as a competitive advantage.

Innovations in Cybersecurity

Emerging technologies such as artificial intelligence (AI), machine learning and Blockchain are reshaping corporate cybersecurity strategies. AI and machine learning can be utilized to predict and identify potential threats faster than traditional methods. These technologies enable real-time threat detection and automated responses, which are the frontline in mitigating the impact of attacks.

Blockchain technology offers a new layer of security due to its decentralized nature and robust encryption, making it particularly useful in securing transactions and reducing fraud. Leaders can leverage these innovations to enhance their cybersecurity frameworks and stay ahead of cybercriminals.

Leaders must also ensure that their organization adopts a Zero-Trust Security Model, defined as a "security framework requiring all users, whether in or outside the organization's network, to be authenticated, authorized, and continuously validated for security configuration and posture before being granted or keeping access to applications and data.[5]"

The nature of executive involvement in cybersecurity will be characterized by the anticipation of sophisticated cyber threats, the adoption of proactive security measures, and the strategic leveraging of technological innovations. As cybersecurity continues to be a critical aspect of business strategy, executives must lead their organizations with foresight, agility and a firm commitment to securing their digital assets and protecting their stakeholders.[3]

Endnotes

1   "Strategic Leadership in Cyber Security," case Finland, ECCWS19-Proceedings1.pdf (aalto.fi), https://www.tandfonline.com/doi/pdf/10.1080/19393555.2020.1813851.

2   IBM Command Center, https://www.ibm.com/blog.

3   "Cybersecurity Starts in the C-Suite: Why Every Role Matters," Business Chief North America. https://businesschief.com/leadership-and--strategy/cybersecurity-what all-c-suite-roles-should-know.

4   https://www.crowdstrike.com/cybersecurity101

5   "Projecting 2024 Cyber Trends and C-Suite Responsibilities," https://www.isaca.org/resources/news-andtrends/newsletters/atisaca/2024/volume-2/projecting-2024-cybertrends-and-csuite-responsibilities.

CHAPTER 3

WHERE DO CYBER THREATS COME FROM?

Cyber threats are many, diverse and malicious. For business leaders, a comprehensive understanding of these threats is essential. This chapter offers a detailed exploration of the types of cyber threats, from the most rudimentary to the highly sophisticated, focusing particularly on phishing attacks, which remain a prevalent and insidious type of cyber assault.

Phishing Attacks

At its core, phishing is fundamentally a game of deception. Cybercriminals craft seemingly legitimate emails, messages or websites to trick individuals into revealing sensitive information such as passwords, credit card numbers, or other information related to their personal identity. These attacks exploit human psychology and manipulate the recipient into performing actions that compromise an organization's security.

Phishing emails may mimic the look and feel of communications from well-known companies, complete with logos and branding that appear authentic at a glance. Links within these messages typically lead to malicious websites that capture login credentials or prompt the download of malware. The success of a phishing attack hinges on the target's reaction to urgent and seemingly legitimate requests for action, such as verifying accounts or confirming passwords.

Spear Phishing

This is a more targeted form of phishing, where the attacker crafts a deceptive message tailored specifically to an individual or an organization itself including websites and public newsletters. By leveraging information that appears relevant and personal—such as details gleaned from social media profiles or organizational websites—spear phishing can be particularly effective. Attackers pose as colleagues, friends or familiar contacts, making requests or claims that exploit the trust the target has in these known entities. The specificity and apparent legitimacy of these communications make spear phishing markedly more dangerous than generic phishing attempts.

Whaling

Aimed specifically at senior executives or other high-profile targets within an organization, whaling is a highly specialized and insidious form of phishing. These attacks are designed to deceive individuals who have significant authority and access within an organization, such as CEOs, CFOs or other top-level executives. The content of a whaling attack is often crafted around executive activities such as wire transfer requests, confidential business deals or legal issues, which adds a layer of plausible urgency and legitimacy to the deception. Due to the potential access and authority of these targets, the consequences of whaling attacks can be particularly damaging, leading to substantial financial losses and severe breaches of corporate security.

To defend against these types of phishing attacks requires implementing security training and awareness programs. Business leaders must lead by example and foster a culture of security mindfulness to protect against these deceptive tactics that target human vulnerabilities as much as technological ones.

Ransomware: Digital Hostage-Taking

Ransomware is an aggressive and direct form of cybersecurity threat that has become increasingly prevalent. It involves malicious software that infiltrates systems and encrypts the victim's data, effectively holding it hostage. Attackers then typically demand a ransom, usually in cryptocurrency, to provide the decryption key. The consequences of ransomware attacks extend far beyond the immediate financial loss of the ransom; they often include substantial operational disruptions, loss of critical data, and long-term reputational damage.

The infiltration process begins when ransomware infects a system through various vectors such as phishing emails, compromised websites or unpatched software vulnerabilities. Once inside the system, the ransomware quickly encrypts files, databases or entire drives, effectively locking out the legitimate users. The sophistication of the encryption used means that without backups or the decryption key, recovering the encrypted data is virtually impossible.

One of the most notorious ransomware attacks was WannaCry in 2017, which affected over 230,000 computers in more than 150 countries. High-profile victims included hospitals, large corporations and government agencies. The malware exploited vulnerabilities in older Windows operating systems. Notably, despite the attackers demanding Bitcoin payments to unlock the affected systems, the quick action of cybersecurity researchers who identified a "kill switch" helped mitigate the attack. This incident highlighted the importance of maintaining updated systems and the effectiveness of prompt, coordinated response strategies.[1]

Impact on Organizations

The impact of a ransomware attack can be devastating. Organizations may face not only the cost of the ransom but also significant operational downtime and potential loss of business. For example, operations can grind to a halt, especially if critical systems are affected, interrupting service delivery and eroding trust among customers and partners. Additionally, organizations must bear the cost of remediation, which involves system restoration, security enhancement and, potentially, legal fees and fines if sensitive information was compromised.

Cryptojacking: A Related Threat

Closely related to ransomware, cryptojacking involves the unauthorized use of someone else's computing resources to mine cryptocurrency. Attackers deploy malware that can take over a victim's computing resources, similar to ransomware. The primary indication that cryptojacking is occurring may be a noticeable slowdown in system performance or an unexpectedly high processor usage.

Like ransomware, the initial infection often stems from phishing or exploiting system vulnerabilities. While cryptojacking does not involve data encryption or demand a ransom, it significantly impacts business operations by slowing down systems and inflating IT costs, especially in terms of power consumption and wear on components.

Proactive Defense Strategies

To defend against ransomware and crypto jacking, organizations must adopt a layered security approach, which includes educating employees about the risks of phishing, regularly updating and patching systems, enforcing strong access controls and maintaining comprehensive backups. Effective response plans that are regularly updated and tested are also crucial to ensure quick recovery from attacks, minimizing downtime and operational impacts.

Distributed Denial of Services

Distributed Denial of Service (DDoS) attacks are among the most disruptive forms of cyber threats faced by organizations today. In a DDoS attack, an overwhelming flood of traffic is directed towards a target system or network, overloading its capacity and causing significant, often catastrophic, service disruptions. These attacks are primarily aimed at crippling websites, online platforms or entire network services, making them inaccessible to legitimate users and disrupting business operations.

DDoS attacks are executed by utilizing a large number of Internet-connected devices, which may include computers, IoT devices and even smartphones. These devices are infected with malware, turning them into bots (or zombies) that can be controlled remotely. The attacker then commands these compromised devices, collectively known as a botnet, to send requests to the target system at the same time. The sheer volume of requests overwhelms the system, leading to service degradation or total outage.

Botnets and Their Role in DDoS Attacks

A botnet is a term that combines "robot" and "network." It is a network of infected computers. Botnets are pernicious, described as "flocks of compromised computers created by software like [the IoT-oriented] Mirai, which then can be used to flood websites with traffic, knocking them offline until ransom is paid."[2] These networks of compromised devices are built over time, and cybercriminals exploit various vulnerabilities in devices' software or use phishing tactics to install malicious software and recruit these devices into their botnets.

A striking example of a massive DDoS attack occurred on October 21, 2016 that targeted Dyn, a company that controls much of the Internet's domain name system (DNS) infrastructure. This attack involved tens of millions of IP addresses and was largely attributed to the Mirai botnet, which spread through Internet-connected devices (the Internet of Things) such as digital cameras and digital video recorders. Dyn estimated that "the attack had involved '100,000 malicious end-points,' and the company … said there had been reports of 'an extraordinary attack strength of 1.2 Tbps,' which is 1.2 trillion bytes per second."[3] Dyn's servers were overwhelmed and the attack caused major Internet platforms and services to become inaccessible across Europe and North America. The fallout highlighted the vulnerability of Internet infrastructure to IoT-driven botnets and underscored the need for improved security practices in IoT devices.[4]

Impact of DDoS Attacks

The impact of DDoS attacks can extend beyond mere operational or technical disruptions. Financially, they can lead to significant losses due to downtime, lost transactions and the cost associated with mitigating the attack and strengthening systems post-incident. Moreover, the reputational damage from failing to protect against such attacks can erode trust among users and customers, potentially leading to a long-term decline in business.

Proactive Defense Strategies

To protect against DDoS attacks, organizations must implement specialized DDoS mitigation tools that can detect and diffuse such attacks before they reach the target servers. Strategies include diversifying the infrastructure to reduce single points of failure, employing cloud-based DDoS protection services that can absorb and disperse large-scale traffic, and establishing strong security protocols for IoT devices to prevent them from becoming part of botnets.

Man-in-the-Middle Attacks

Man-in-the-Middle (MitM) attacks represent a significant threat in the realm of network security. These attacks occur when an attacker secretly intercepts and potentially alters the communications between two parties without their knowledge. The objective can range from eavesdropping on private conversations to stealing sensitive data or injecting malicious content into the communication stream. The implications of such breaches can be severe, involving loss of privacy, data theft and compromised integrity of information.

MitM attacks typically exploit vulnerabilities in the communication protocols between devices or between a user and a network. Attackers may position themselves in a network or use malware to reroute communications through a device they control. Common techniques include ARP spoofing, which manipulates address resolution protocol data to intercept network traffic, and SSL stripping, which downgrades a secure HTTPS connection to a less secure HTTP connection, making it easier to intercept transmitted data.

Session Hijacking: A Common Form of MitM

One prevalent form of MitM attack is session hijacking. In this scenario, the attacker exploits a valid computer session—the session key—to gain unauthorized access to information or services within a computer system. For instance, an attacker might capture the session token of a user's login to a financial service website; with this token, the attacker can impersonate the user and authorize transactions, or alter account information.

In 2015, hackers conducted a sophisticated attack on Premera Blue Cross that began with a phishing email to the company's employees. Once the attackers gained a foothold, they were able to move laterally within the network and use MitM tactics to intercept and manipulate data being transmitted between different nodes within the network. This breach ultimately exposed the sensitive personal, financial and medical information of over 11 million customers. The incident led to significant financial losses due to regulatory fines and settlements, and in addition severely damaged the company's reputation.[5]

Impact and Mitigation of MitM Attacks

MitM attacks compromise the confidentiality and integrity of sensitive communications and data. It's also the case that businesses can suffer financial losses and legal repercussions, as well as damage to customer relationships. To mitigate the risk of MitM attacks, organizations should implement strong encryption protocols for data transmissions, use HTTPS for all their web interactions, and employ endpoint security measures that detect and prevent the installation of any malicious software that could reroute communications. Additionally, educating employees about the risks of phishing and other tactics that could give attackers initial access is crucial.

Organizations need to adopt a layered security approach to effectively defend against MitM attacks. This includes regular security assessments to identify and mitigate vulnerabilities in network infrastructure, robust authentication mechanisms to prevent unauthorized access, and continuous monitoring of network traffic for anomalies that may indicate an ongoing MitM attack.

Advanced Persistent Threats

Advanced Persistent Threats (APTs) represent a category of cyber threats characterized by their stealthy, prolonged presence within a target's network. These threats are often state-sponsored or launched by organized crime and aim to steal sensitive data, conduct espionage or sabotage systems. APTs are notorious for their sophistication and the complexity of their tactics, which include gaining deep access to networks and maintaining that access undetected over extended periods.

APTs are typically initiated through common vectors like phishing or exploiting network vulnerabilities. Once access is gained, unlike other cyber threats that seek quick hits or immediate financial gain, APTs nestle into a system to systematically gather valuable data. The key to their persistence lies in their ability to remain undetected, often using legitimate credentials and mimicking normal network activities to avoid raising alarms. Think of an APT as a "chronic infection rather than a transitory attack, as espionage and embezzlement rather than burglary, as an invasion and occupation rather than a hit-and-run raid."[6]

One of the most critical aspects of APTs is lateral movement, the technique used by attackers to navigate through a network in search of more valuable data or targets after the initial entry. This movement involves escalating privileges or exploiting system vulnerabilities to gain access to additional systems and data repositories across the network. Lateral movement is typically stealthy and can be challenging to detect because it may occur slowly and mimic legitimate user activities.

A prominent example of an APT in action is the 2015 data breach of Anthem Inc., one of the largest health insurance companies in the U.S. Cyber attackers, believed to be part of a state-sponsored group from

China, gained unauthorized access to Anthem's IT system and exfiltrated personal information belonging to approximately 78.8 million people.

The attackers initially gained access through a phishing email that led to the deployment of malware on the network. Once inside, they used sophisticated techniques to move laterally across the network, ultimately reaching the database that contained vast amounts of personal and medical information. The breach was not detected for several weeks, highlighting the stealthy nature of APTs and the difficulty in detecting such threats without sophisticated monitoring tools.

Impact and Mitigation of APT Attacks

The impact of APTs like the Anthem breach can be devastating due to the scale of information loss and the potential for significant financial and reputational damage. To defend against APTs, organizations need to implement a multi-layered security strategy that includes regular system audits, the use of advanced threat detection tools, and rigorous staff training on security best practices. Networks should be segmented to limit lateral movement possibilities; in addition, strict access controls should be enforced to minimize the number of users with access to sensitive data.

Real-time monitoring and behavioral analysis tools can also play a role in detecting unusual activities that might indicate the presence of an APT actor within the network. These tools can help identify patterns that deviate from normal operations, potentially flagging malicious activities before they lead to data loss or damage.

Zero-Day Exploits

Zero-day exploits represent a nefarious threat due to their nature and timing. These attacks target vulnerabilities in software that are unknown to the software vendor and, therefore, unpatched. This gives cybercriminals a significant advantage, as they exploit these vulnerabilities before developers have a chance to issue fixes, leaving systems exposed and defenseless. The period between the discovery of the vulnerability and the release of a patch is a window of opportunity for attackers to cause maximum disruption or steal valuable data.

The term "zero-day" refers to the fact that the developers have zero days to fix the vulnerability upon its discovery because the exploit occurs as soon as the vulnerability becomes known to the public, and sometimes even before. These vulnerabilities can be found in any software, including operating systems, browsers or even security software. Hackers might use zero-day exploits to inject malware, steal data or gain unauthorized access to systems.

A notable case of a zero-day exploit is the Stuxnet worm, discovered in 2010, which targeted industrial control systems used in Iran's nuclear program. Stuxnet exploited four zero-day vulnerabilities in Microsoft Windows and Siemens' PCS 7, WinCC and STEP7 industrial software applications. The worm was able to spread across networks, seek out specific Siemens software and reprogram programmable logic controllers to induce the destruction of centrifuges at nuclear facilities.

This sophisticated attack not only demonstrated the potential for significant physical and operational damage through cyber means, but also highlighted the challenges in defending against zero-day exploits, especially when multiple zero-days are used in conjunction. The development and deployment of Stuxnet required extensive knowledge of industrial processes, suggesting the involvement of state-sponsored actors with substantial resources.

Impact and Mitigation of Zero-Day Exploit Attacks

The impact of zero-day exploits range from financial losses and operational downtime to severe damage to critical infrastructure and national security. To mitigate these threats, organizations must adopt comprehensive security measures that include not only regular updates and patch management but also advanced threat detection systems and strong security protocols.

One such security protocol is patch management which involves regularly updating and patching software vulnerabilities as soon as patches become available. This practice is essential in defending against known vulnerabilities, but it also plays a significant role in mitigating the impact of zero-day attacks by ensuring that all other potential vulnerabilities are addressed promptly, reducing the overall attack surface.

* * *

Employing security solutions that use behavioral analysis and anomaly detection can help identify unusual activity that might indicate an exploit in progress, even if the specific vulnerability is not yet known. Moreover, maintaining a rigorous regime of vulnerability assessments and penetration testing can help identify and shore up potential weaknesses before they can be exploited.

We've explored a range of cyber threats—from the deceptive simplicity of phishing attacks to the complex and hidden dangers of Advanced Persistent Threats (APTs) and zero-day exploits. The better informed business leaders are about these threats, the better able they are to strategize their cybersecurity defenses, ensuring their organization is prepared to anticipate and effectively respond to these threats.

As we move forward, the next chapter, we'll shift our focus from understanding specific threats to examining comprehensive strategies and practices that enhance an organization's overall resilience against cyberattacks. This progression is essential for developing dynamic defenses against cyber threats while supporting long-term organizational sustainability and success.

Endnotes

1 WannaCry ransomware attack. See Wikipedia, https://en.wikipedia.org/wiki/WannaCry_ransomware_attack.

2 Rothrock, 197.

3 Rothrock, 33.

4 DDoS attacks on Dyn. See Wikipedia, https://en.wikipedia.org/wiki/DDoS_attacks_on_Dyn.

5 "Premera Blue Cross Breach Exposes Financial, Medical Records," Krebs on Security, https://krebsonsecurity.com/2015/03/premera-blue-cross-breach-exposes-financial-medical-records/.

6 Digital Resilience, 8.

CHAPTER 4

BUILDING A
CYBER-RESILIENT ORGANIZATION

Cyber resilience refers to an organization's capacity to anticipate, withstand, recover from and adapt to adverse cyber events. Building a cyber-resilient organization requires a comprehensive and proactive approach that encompasses technology, processes and people. Organizations must integrate cybersecurity awareness into their core values and operational procedures. This chapter explores the multifaceted strategies and steps involved in enhancing an organization's resilience against cyberattacks.

Risk Assessment: Identifying Vulnerabilities

A fundamental step in building cyber resilience is conducting thorough risk assessments. This process involves identifying, analyzing and evaluating potential vulnerabilities within an organization's systems and processes—both human and non-human elements. By identifying where vulnerabilities lie, organizations can implement targeted defenses more effectively.

One process to help discover vulnerabilities is vulnerability scanning which, done on a regular basis, helps to maintain an up-to-date awareness of potential weak points within IT systems. This can be conducted using specialized software tools that systematically check for known vulnerabilities, such as outdated software, misconfigurations and unpatched systems. These tools provide a dynamic view of an organization's exposure to risk, enabling IT teams to address vulnerabilities before they can be exploited by cybercriminals.

In addition, threat modeling is a process of identifying potential threat actors, their motivations and the methods they might use to target an organization. This process helps in crafting a defensive strategy that is not just reactive but anticipative. By considering various attack scenarios, organizations can prepare and implement more effective security measures tailored to the specific risks they face.

The cyberattack on Sony Pictures Entertainment in 2014 underscores the importance of cyber-resilience. Hackers breached Sony's network and released confidential data, including personal information about employees and high-profile email exchanges. The attack not only caused a significant and immediate disruption, but also had long-lasting reputational and financial impacts.[1]

This incident highlighted lapses in Sony's cybersecurity practices, particularly in areas of risk assessment and internal communications security. In response, Sony had to overhaul its cybersecurity framework, which involved not only upgrading its digital defenses but also enhancing its organizational structure to better manage and respond to cyber threats. This example demonstrates the need for continuous risk assessment and adaptive security practices as part of a holistic approach to building cyber-resilience.

Cybersecurity Is a Shared Responsibility

As we investigate building cyber-resilience capacity, it becomes clear that beyond just safeguarding against potential threats, organizations must instill a culture where cybersecurity is a shared responsibility. This involves training all employees to be vigilant and informed about cyber risks, implementing strong policies and procedures, and ensuring that cybersecurity measures evolve in step with changing threat landscapes and technological advancements.

Have an Incident Response Plan

An effective incident response plan goes a long way for any organization aiming to manage and mitigate the impact of cyber incidents swiftly and efficiently. In the face of a cyberattack, the difference between a minor disruption and a major catastrophe often lies in how well-prepared an organization is with a clear and actionable incident response plan. This section outlines the essential components of such a plan, emphasizing the importance of predefined roles, responsibilities and communication protocols.

Defining Roles and Responsibilities

The first step in crafting an incident response plan is to clearly define the roles and responsibilities of the incident response team. This clarity ensures that during a cyber incident, every team member knows their specific duties and can act without hesitation. Key roles typically include:

An incident manager who oversees and coordinates the response to ensure the incident is handled efficiently.

Security analysts and technical responders who work on the technical front to identify the breach's scope, contain the incident, eradicate the threat and ensures the organization recovers from the attack.

A **communications officer** who manages all communications, both internal and external, during the incident.

Legal advisors who provide advice on the legal implications of the incident and liaises with law enforcement if necessary.

Communication Protocols

Effective communication during and after a cyber incident is paramount. The incident response plan should specify how information about the incident will be communicated within the organization and to external parties. This includes:

Internal communication to ensure that all relevant internal stakeholders are kept informed about the incident's status and actions being taken. This helps in maintaining order and preventing the spread of unverified information.

External communication that outlines how and when to notify external stakeholders, including customers, partners, regulatory bodies and the media. This is necessary not only for compliance with data breach notification laws but also for maintaining public trust and managing the organization's reputation.

The 2013 Target Data Breach

In December 2013, Target, one of the largest retailers in the U.S., experienced a massive data breach in which the personal and payment information of approximately 40 million customers was compromised. The breach occurred when hackers gained access to Target's network using credentials stolen from a third-party vendor.[2] This breach not only exposed sensitive customer data but also had significant financial repercussions, including a settlement of over $18 million with affected states and an estimated total cost of nearly $202 million.[3]

In the Target breach, there were significant delays in understanding the scope and shutting down the breach. This highlighted a need for clear roles and rapid action protocols, which were found lacking. The breach underscored the importance of having a dedicated incident response team that is well-trained and ready to act as soon as a breach is detected.

One of the major criticisms faced by Target was related to its (mis) handling of public communications following the breach. Initially, there was a delay in notifying affected customers and the public, which damaged trust and heightened customer frustration. This case illustrates the need for an incident response plan that includes prompt, transparent and effective communication strategies to manage public relations and legal considerations effectively.

The Target breach serves as a cautionary tale for other organizations on the importance of:

- ensuring that every aspect of the incident response plan is actionable and that roles are clearly defined to avoid confusion during a crisis;

- implementing stringent security measures for both the organization and its network of vendors to prevent similar attacks; and

- developing a communication strategy that addresses both internal stakeholders and the public quickly and transparently to maintain trust and manage the narrative.

From the Target example, it is clear that comprehensive incident response planning is crucial not just for managing the technical aspects of a security breach but also for handling customer relations and regulatory compliance effectively.

Regular Training Empowers Employees as Cyber Defenders

In the battle against cyber threats, an organization's employees can indeed be its strongest defense or its weakest link. Regular and comprehensive training equips employees with the necessary knowledge and tools to protect the organization's digital assets effectively. This training involves not only raising awareness about the latest threats and best practices, but also actively testing and reinforcing these practices through simulated drills.

Conduct Awareness Campaigns

One of the most effective ways to maintain cybersecurity at the forefront of your employees' minds is through ongoing awareness campaigns. These campaigns should inform staff about the latest cybersecurity threats and the best practices for mitigating these risks. Methods to deliver this critical information can vary, including digital newsletters, interactive workshops or educational seminars. The key is to keep the content engaging and relevant, ensuring that all employees, regardless of their technical background, can understand and apply the lessons to their daily work. Regular updates play a role in keeping security practices fresh and top of mind. By consistently communicating the importance of cybersecurity and updating employees on new and evolving threats, organizations can foster a culture of security awareness that permeates throughout the workplace.

Conduct Simulated Drills

Simulated cyber-incident drills are an invaluable part of any cybersecurity training program. These drills involve creating scenarios in which employees must respond to a simulated attack or breach. The purpose of these exercises is to test the effectiveness of both individual and collective response strategies and to identify any gaps in knowledge or preparedness.

During these simulations, organizations can assess critical aspects such as the speed and appropriateness of the response, the effectiveness of communication among team members, and the ability of employees to apply their training in a high-pressure situation. Feedback from these drills can then be used to refine procedures and training programs, enhancing the overall security posture of the organization.

The Maersk Notpetya Attack

In June 2017, A.P. Moller-Maersk, one of the world's largest shipping companies, was hit by the NotPetya malware attack. This cyberattack was devastating in its scope and impact, affecting Maersk's global operations and leading to considerable financial and operational disruptions. The malware, initially targeting organizations in Ukraine, spread globally and caused widespread damage to the unprepared networks of many multinational corporations, including Maersk.[4]

NotPetya was designed to spread rapidly across networks by exploiting vulnerabilities in Microsoft Windows systems. Once inside, it encrypted data on computers, rendering them inoperative and demanding a ransom to unlock the data. At Maersk, this resulted in the shutdown of IT systems across multiple sites and business units, including container operations and port terminal operations. The company estimated the total cost of the incident at around US$300 million due to direct system outages, disruption in operations, and recovery efforts.

Post-attack, Maersk took significant steps to recover its operations and bolster its cybersecurity defenses. Maersk implemented comprehensive cybersecurity training for its employees, emphasizing the importance of security practices and how to recognize potential cyber threats. The training included detailed sessions on the nature of malware attacks, phishing and other common cyber threats, along with practical advice on how to prevent them. Employees were trained on the importance of maintaining software updates and using strong, unique passwords. Regular simulated cyber drills were introduced to ensure that employees could not only recognize the signs of a cyberattack but also react swiftly and effectively in accordance with established incident response protocols.

In addition, simulated drills became a regular activity at Maersk, designed to test and improve the company's incident response capabilities. These exercises have allowed the company to assess the effectiveness of its communication protocols during an incident, the decision-making process under pressure, and the overall readiness of their teams to handle unexpected cybersecurity events.

The NotPetya attack on Maersk serves as an example of how severe cyberattacks can be and the critical role of employee training in an organization's cybersecurity strategy. By investing in regular training and simulated drills, Maersk not only enhanced its resilience against future attacks but also fostered a corporate culture deeply aware of and prepared for cybersecurity challenges. This case underlines the necessity for continuous employee education and proactive security practices to safeguard against the evolving landscape of cyber threats.

Backup Systems: How to Ensure Data Integrity and Availability

Data is often described as the lifeblood of modern organizations, making data protection a huge priority. Backup initiatives are not only about preserving data, but also guaranteeing the availability and integrity of data under all circumstances, including cyberattacks or other disasters.

For any organization, backup systems are meant to maintain business continuity with minimal disruption, and preserve organizational functions and customer trust. The strategic approach to backups should be comprehensive and involve both offsite storage and regular testing to ensure data can be effectively restored when needed. By adopting rigorous backup strategies, organizations can protect themselves against a variety of threats and ensure that their data remains intact and available, thereby safeguarding their operations and the trust of their customers and partners

Offsite Backups

One fundamental aspect of a dynamic backup strategy is the use of offsite backups. Storing backup data in a geographically separate location from the primary data center cannot be overemphasized. Offsite backups can be managed through cloud storage services or at physically distant data centers, providing organizations with the assurance that whatever happens at the primary site, the data remains secure and accessible elsewhere.

Conduct Regular Testing of Backups

Merely having backup systems in place is not enough. Regular testing of these backups is required to ensure they function correctly when needed. This testing should involve not only verifying the integrity of the backup data but also of the restoration process. It ensures that the data can be quickly and accurately restored to operational status without significant delays or issues, which is critical during a cyber incident recovery phase.

The GitHub DDoS Attack

In 2018, GitHub, one of the largest code-hosting platforms in the world, faced a massive distributed denial-of-service (DDoS) attack. The attack peaked at 1.35 Tbps, making it one of the largest of its kind at the time. Due to GitHub's proactive cybersecurity measures and robust backup systems, the platform was able to thwart the attack and recover without significant data loss.[5]

GitHub's strategy included comprehensive offsite backups and regular testing regimes, which ensured the company could quickly restore any affected data and maintain service continuity. Its backup and recovery systems were part of a broader disaster recovery plan that included immediate automated responses to threats. GitHub's effective handling of the DDoS attack highlights the importance of having well-prepared backup systems that are regularly tested and capable of responding to both cyber and physical threats.

Continuous Monitoring: The Key to Proactive Cybersecurity

Organizations can use advanced monitoring tools to help identify and mitigate threats before they can cause significant damage. This section will explore critical tools such as Intrusion Detection Systems (IDS) and Security Information and Event Management (SIEM) solutions, which are essential for a continuous monitoring strategy.

Intrusion Detection Systems

IDS are essential for monitoring network traffic and identifying suspicious activities that could indicate a cyberattack. These systems work by analyzing traffic to recognize patterns or signatures that match known threats, or by identifying deviations from normal activity patterns, which might suggest an intrusion. When potential threats are detected, IDS alerts system administrators, providing them with information needed to take prompt corrective action.

Security Information and Event Management

SIEM solutions offer a more comprehensive approach by collecting and analyzing data from various sources across an organization's IT infrastructure. This includes logs from servers, network devices, applications and security systems. By aggregating this data, SIEM tools provide a holistic view of the organization's security posture, enabling IT teams to detect patterns and anomalies that could indicate a cyber threat. SIEM systems are not only designed for threat detection, but also for incident response and compliance management, as they can automate responses to certain types of incidents and generate reports that aid in meeting regulatory requirements.

The Sony PlayStation Network Attack

A relevant example of the important role of continuous monitoring can be found in the 2011 attack on Sony's PlayStation Network. This cyberattack resulted in the theft of personal information from approximately 77 million accounts. The breach exposed significant vulnerabilities in Sony's network, particularly in its monitoring capabilities.[6]

Post-attack analyses suggested that enhanced continuous monitoring systems could have detected unusual network traffic and potentially prevented the extensive damage caused by the breach. Following the incident, Sony undertook a major overhaul of its cybersecurity infrastructure, which included significant upgrades to its continuous monitoring and intrusion detection capabilities. The company implemented a comprehensive SIEM system that enhanced its ability to detect and respond to incidents more rapidly and effectively.

This attack underscores the necessity for continuous monitoring within an organization's cybersecurity strategy. By implementing IDS and SIEM systems, organizations can enhance their ability to detect and respond to threats in real time, thereby safeguarding their digital assets against sophisticated cyberattacks. This proactive approach is essential for any organization looking to maintain resilience in the face of the constantly evolving landscape of cyber threats.

* * *

We've explored essential strategies that fortify an organization's defenses against the persistent and evolving threats of the digital world. From comprehensive risk assessments and incident response planning to regular employee training and robust backup systems, each component plays a significant role in enhancing an organization's ability to not only withstand cyberattacks but also recover from them effectively. We have also examined the practice of continuous monitoring, which ensures that potential security threats are identified and addressed promptly.

In the next chapter the focus is on the implementation of these strategies within the framework of continuous training and fostering a culture of cybersecurity awareness within an organization. We will (1) highlight the necessity of empowering every member of an organization with the knowledge and tools they need to contribute positively to cybersecurity efforts, and (2) explore strategies for developing ongoing training programs and awareness campaigns. Such campaigns not only educate employees about their roles in preventing cyber incidents but also nurture a culture of security-mindedness across all levels of the organization. This focus on the human element is crucial for creating a comprehensive and resilient cybersecurity posture.

ENDNOTES

1   2014 Sony Pictures hack. See Wikipedia, https://en.wikipedia.org/wiki/2014_Sony_Pictures_hack.

2 "How hackers stole millions of credit card records from Target," ZDNET 1701.04940.pdf, https://www.zdnet.com/article/howhackers-stole-millions-of-credit-card-records-from-target/.

3   NBC News, "Target Settles 2013 Hacked Customer Data Breach for $18.5 Million." https://www.nbcnews.com/business/business-news/target-settles-2013-hacked-customer-data-breach-18-5-million-n764031.

4 "Ransomware: The key lesson Maersk learned from battling the Not-Petya attack," ZDNET, https://www.zdnet.com/article/ransomware-the-key-lesson-maersk-learned-from-battling-the-notpetyaattack/#-google_vignette.

5 "DDoS Incident Report," The GitHub blog, https://github.blog/2018-03-01-ddos-incident-report/.

6 2011 PlayStation Network outage. See Wikipedia, https://en.wikipedia.org/wiki/2011_PlayStation_Network_outage.

CHAPTER 5

THE HUMAN ELEMENT IN CYBERSECURITY

While the integrity of technology is critical, so is the integrity of the human domain. Employees act as both the first line of defense and potentially the most significant vulnerability within an organization. The question is, how can an organization build a cybersecurity-first culture?

This chapter describes the elements of a culture of cybersecurity that ensures every individual, from the CEO to the newest intern, understands and embraces their role in safeguarding the organization's digital assets. Cybersecurity is not the sole domain of the IT department; it is a collective responsibility that extends across every part of an organization. Everyone plays a crucial role, whether they handle data directly, manage systems, or simply use network resources in their daily job functions. Emphasizing this shared responsibility helps to cultivate a mindset where cybersecurity becomes a fundamental aspect of organizational culture. To that end, regular training sessions, comprehensive onboarding processes, and continuous communications can help reinforce the message that security is a critical aspect of everyone's job description.

Managers must be accountable for providing regular feedback on cybersecurity practices. This is best done in regular check-ins or when opportunities arise to discuss cybersecurity tactics. Feedback should focus not only on areas for improvement but also acknowledge and reward compliance and proactive behavior. This approach ensures that cybersecurity remains a focal point of employee performance considerations, keeping it at the forefront of organizational priorities.

Feedback mechanisms can also include the use of cybersecurity audits, where employees' practices are reviewed to ensure they align with the organization's policies and standards. The results from these audits can then be discussed in one-on-one sessions, offering personalized guidance and support to help employees improve their security behaviors.

At the end of the chapter is a case study about IBM, which serves to illustrate the points raised through the chapter.

Cultivate a Cyber-Aware Workforce

Employee Training

The importance of continuous education in cybersecurity cannot be overstated. A cyber-aware workforce is essential for identifying and responding to threats effectively. Training should not be viewed as a one-time event, but as an ongoing and evolving process that is intended to keep pace with the rapidly changing landscape of cyber threats. It should also be mandatory for new hires.

The onboarding process should cover the organization's cybersecurity policies, the employee's specific role in maintaining cybersecurity, and an overview of common cyber threats. Setting this tone from day one emphasizes the seriousness with which the organization views cybersecurity.

Because technology continues to advance and as cybercriminals become more sophisticated, the need for a knowledgeable and vigilant workforce has become a baseline requirement. This lays the groundwork for transforming the human element from a potential liability into a key asset in cybersecurity defense. By embracing continuous education and fostering a culture of cybersecurity awareness, organizations can significantly enhance their overall security posture.

In addition to training employees on a regular basis, holding periodic refresher courses also pays dividends. Refresher sessions can be held quarterly or bi-annually and should educate employees on new and emerging threats, as well as provide updates to the company's cybersecurity policies and procedures. This ongoing training ensures that all employees, regardless of their seniority or hierarchical level, remain knowledgeable and vigilant about protecting the organization's digital assets.

PhishMe (now Cofense), a leading provider of phishing defense solutions, exemplifies the effective implementation of regular training and awareness programs. Recognizing that employees can be a first line of defense against phishing attempts, PhishMe developed simulation-based training focused on recognizing phishing emails. This approach not only educates employees about the specifics of identifying phishing attempts, but also regularly tests their knowledge in a practical, engaging way.

The results were telling. Over time, PhishMe's approach helped reduce the susceptibility of employees to phishing attacks dramatically, turning them from the weakest link into a strong, proactive component of the organization's cybersecurity defense. Their success story emphasizes the power of continuous, practical training in enhancing cybersecurity awareness and response capabilities across an organization.

Conduct Simulated Attacks

While theoretical knowledge lays the foundation for understanding cybersecurity, practical experience through simulated attacks is invaluable for testing and improving an organization's real-world readiness. These simulations help bridge the gap between knowing what to do and being able to do it effectively under pressure. They provide not only a test of the organization's defenses, but also serve as crucial teaching moments that can dramatically increase the cybersecurity competence of its workforce.

Conduct Mock Phishing Attacks

One of the most effective ways to enhance cybersecurity awareness and preparedness is through mock phishing attacks. These are controlled exercises where realistic, but innocuous, phishing emails are crafted and sent to employees to gauge their reactions. This method tests employees' ability to identify suspicious emails based on their training and instinct.

For those who fall for the mock phishing attempts, these exercises provide immediate, impactful learning opportunities. Feedback is provided in a constructive manner, helping employees understand what cues they missed and how they can improve their vigilance. Regular mock phishing attacks keep employees alert, reinforce training materials, and help cybersecurity teams assess the ongoing effectiveness of their educational programs.[1]

Employ Red Team Exercises

Red team exercises involve engaging teams of cybersecurity professionals to simulate a full-scale, real-world attack on an organization's defenses. Unlike mock phishing, which tests individual employee awareness, red team exercises are comprehensive evaluations of an organization's entire readiness—encompassing both its technical defenses and the human responses to attacks.

These exercises are designed to mimic the tactics, techniques and procedures used by actual attackers, providing a rigorous test of all aspects of an organization's cybersecurity protocols. Red team exercises help identify vulnerabilities in both infrastructure and response strategies, offering valuable insights that can be used to strengthen security measures.

Simulated attacks like mock phishing and red team exercises are critical components of an effective cybersecurity strategy. They provide employees and management with practical, hands-on experience and help identify and rectify vulnerabilities in an organization's defenses. By regularly incorporating these simulations, organizations can ensure that their teams are not only aware of the best practices in cybersecurity but are also adept at applying them in real-world scenarios. This hands-on approach is vital for developing a truly resilient organization, ready to face the challenges posed by evolving cyber threats.

The JPMorgan Chase Red Team Exercise

A notable example of effective use of red team exercises can be seen with JPMorgan Chase, one of the largest banks in the United States. Following a significant breach in 2014, JPMorgan increased its cybersecurity budget and implemented regular red team exercises to ensure its systems and employees were prepared to handle sophisticated cyber threats. These exercises led to a heightened state of readiness and helped the bank develop a more proactive approach to cybersecurity.[2]

During one such exercise, JPMorgan's red team employed tactics that mimicked a potential intruder's approach, attempting to breach the company's financial systems and access high-value data. The exercise revealed several critical insights into how real attackers could exploit both system vulnerabilities and human factors. The results were used to further tighten security measures and refine response protocols, significantly enhancing the bank's overall cyber resilience.

The Role of Clear Communication in Cybersecurity Measures

In the intricate realm of cybersecurity, ensuring that all employees understand what to do and whom to contact when they encounter or suspect a cyber threat is crucial for maintaining robust cybersecurity defenses. Strategies to enhance clear communication include maintaining an open-door policy and establishing effective feedback loops, which together foster a proactive and responsive cybersecurity culture.

The Open-Door Policy

An open-door policy in cybersecurity encourages employees to report any suspicious activity or potential threats without fear of repercussions. This policy removes any hesitation on an employee's part to report an incident for fear of making a false report or be held accountable for a suspected incident. By fostering an environment where open communication is supported and encouraged, organizations can significantly increase the likelihood of early detection of potential threats. Early detection is often the key to preventing a minor security concern from escalating into a major breach.

Implementing an open-door policy requires not only clear communication from leadership about its importance but also regular reminders of the policy's existence and purpose. Training sessions should emphasize the importance of reporting and the procedures for doing so. Ensuring that all employees know the specific steps to take and whom to contact makes it more likely that they will engage with the process.

Use a Feedback Loop

When an employee reports a potential threat, their manager must close the loop with them. Providing feedback on the outcome of their report serves multiple functions: it reinforces the importance of their action (and establishes whether the threat was genuine or a false alarm), and it encourages continued vigilance and participation in the cybersecurity protocols of the organization. Feedback ensures that employees feel valued and understand that their proactive behavior has a direct impact on the safety of the organization.

Providing detailed feedback can also be educational. For instance, if a report turns out to be a false alarm, explaining why can help employees better understand what to look for and how to differentiate between malicious and benign activities. Conversely, if a report uncovers a genuine threat, sharing this information can serve as a powerful reminder of the critical role that every employee plays in cybersecurity.

Clear communication supported by an open-door policy and effective feedback loops cultivate a proactive cybersecurity culture. These strategies ensure that employees are not only well-informed and prepared to act, but also feel supported and valued in their role as key players in defending the organization.

A pertinent case study highlighting the importance of clear communication and feedback is the response of Salesforce to a phishing scam incident. In 2015, Salesforce detected a targeted phishing campaign aimed at compromising customer information. The company immediately communicated the incident to its customers, explaining the nature of the threat, the steps Salesforce was taking to address it, and how customers could protect themselves.

Moreover, Salesforce maintained a transparent communication line with all stakeholders throughout the incident and provided updates on the resolution and outcomes of their investigations. This not only helped in mitigating the impact of the attack but also strengthened trust in their security processes.[3]

Reward and Recognition: Motivating Cybersecurity Vigilance

In any organization, fostering a culture that promotes and rewards exemplary behavior can significantly enhance employee motivation and performance, especially in critical areas like cybersecurity. Positive reinforcement through reward and recognition programs is a powerful tool to encourage employees to maintain high standards of cybersecurity vigilance. These initiatives not only acknowledge individual contributions but also serve to elevate the importance of cybersecurity across the entire organization.

One effective approach to recognizing and rewarding diligent cybersecurity practices is through an Employee of the Month program focused on cybersecurity. Such recognition not only acknowledges individuals who have demonstrated an exceptional commitment to cybersecurity protocols, but also sets a benchmark for other employees to strive for. It sends a clear message about the organization's serious stance on cybersecurity and the value placed on proactive behavior. This program can be structured to recognize various actions, such as reporting phishing attempts, suggesting improvements to security protocols, or helping to educate fellow employees about security best practices. Highlighting these behaviors in company newsletters, on internal social media or during staff meetings can amplify the message and encourage a widespread culture of security.

Beyond recognition, tangible incentives can further enhance motivation. Implementing incentive programs that reward employees for consistently demonstrating cybersecurity best practices can be highly effective. These rewards might include gift cards, bonuses, extra vacation days or even public acknowledgment in company communications. For example, a company could offer a quarterly bonus to the department that scores the highest in cybersecurity compliance audits or provide gift cards to employees who complete additional cybersecurity training courses. Such incentives not only boost morale but also encourage a continuous, active engagement with cybersecurity initiatives.

An example of such an approach is Google's Vulnerability Reward Program (VRP). The VRP targets a broad community including external security researchers; however, the principles of the program can be adapted to an internal corporate environment. Google's VRP offers financial rewards to individuals who report vulnerabilities in Google's software products.[4] Since its inception, the program has been highly successful in identifying and mitigating potential security threats before they could be exploited maliciously. Google's approach demonstrates the effectiveness of financial incentives in promoting security-focused behavior.

As we proceed to explore further into creating dynamic cybersecurity frameworks, the role of such positive reinforcement mechanisms becomes even more pivotal in ensuring that cybersecurity is seen not just as a necessity but as a shared responsibility and opportunity for recognition within the company.

IBM's Security Culture

IBM provides a prime example of how embedding a culture of accountability can enhance an organization's cybersecurity posture. Known for its advanced cybersecurity frameworks, IBM emphasizes security as a core component of its operational ethos. The company has instituted a comprehensive cybersecurity education program for all its employees, which is continually updated to address emerging threats and technology evolutions. IBM also practices regular security audits and uses the results as part of its employee appraisal process. By doing so, IBM not only maintains high security standards, but also fosters an environment where employees are motivated to excel in their security practices. The company's approach demonstrates that when employees are held accountable and provided with consistent feedback, the entire organization's security stance is strengthened.

* * *

Creating a culture of accountability in cybersecurity is essential for protecting an organization's digital assets. By ensuring that every employee understands their role in cybersecurity, and by regularly reinforcing this responsibility through feedback and recognition, organizations can significantly enhance their defensive capabilities. This culture of shared responsibility and continuous improvement is crucial for maintaining resilience against an ever-evolving array of cyber threats. As cyber expert Ray A. Rothrock writes, "The resilience of a physical structure depends on the resilience of the individual components with which it is built. The resilience of an organization depends on the individual resilience of its members. … Even resilient people make mistakes, whether they are building a digital network or designing an organization."[5] Organizations must remain vigilant against the exploitation of personal information of their employees through training and education.

In the next chapter, our focus shifts to technical strategies and frameworks that are essential for securing digital assets. This involves implementing security protocols to bolster an organization's technological defenses through integrating human vigilance and technical resilience.

Endnotes

1 "How to Run an Effective Phishing Test at Work," Dashlane blog, https://www.dashlane.com/blog/phishing-test.

2 "What Is a Red Team Exercise & Why Should You Conduct One?" https://www.kroll.com/en/insights/publications/cyber/why-conduct-a-red-team-exercise/.

3 "Phishing and Malware," *Salesforce Security Guide*, Salesforce Developers Salesforce Trust, https://developer.salesforce.com/docs/atlas.enus.securityImplGuide.meta/securityImplGuide/security_overview_trust.htm.

4 "Google and Alphabet Vulnerability Reward Program (VRP) Rules," Google Bug Hunters, https://bughunters.google.com/about/rules/6625378258649088/google-and-alphabet-vulnerability-reward-program-vrp-rules.

5 Rothrock, 72.

CHAPTER 6

IMPLEMENTING ROBUST SECURITY PROTOCOLS

Robust security protocols such as multi-factor authentication, updating software on a regular basis, and implementing firewalls and intrusion detection systems form the backbone of an organization's defense strategy. This chapter describes those protocols and how they can be implemented to enhance security.

Multi-Factor Authentication

Multi-Factor Authentication (MFA) is a security measure that requires users to provide multiple forms of verification before they can be granted access to systems or data. This additional layer of security significantly reduces the risk of unauthorized access, as it makes it much harder for attackers to breach systems with just a stolen password.

MFA integrates two or more independent credentials: something you know (such as a password or PIN), something you have (such as a smart card, a security token or a mobile device app), and something unique to your person (e.g., utilizing biometrics like fingerprints or facial recognition). By combining these different forms of evidence, MFA creates a dynamic defense mechanism that can adapt to various security needs.

To maximize the effectiveness of MFA, it must be rolled out across all systems, and particularly those systems which are accessible remotely. This includes administrative interfaces, cloud-based platforms and systems containing sensitive or proprietary information. Best practices for implementing MFA include:

Comprehensive Coverage: Ensure MFA is applied not only to external access points but also internally, especially for access to data centers and high-impact information systems;

Regular Updates and Testing: Continuously update the authentication mechanisms to address new security threats. Regular testing of the MFA system is essential to ensure it remains effective against evolving cybersecurity challenges; and

User Education and Support: Provide training and resources to help users understand the importance of MFA and how to use it effectively. Support should be readily available to address any issues that arise during its use.

Implementing security protocols like MFA is an essential strategy for enhancing an organization's cybersecurity posture. As we continue to explore other critical security protocols, the importance of integrating comprehensive, well-managed security measures becomes increasingly apparent.

The Github MFA Implementation

GitHub is one of the largest code hosting platforms in the world. Faced with increasing security challenges, GitHub rolled out mandatory MFA for its contributors to protect against unauthorized access to repositories and sensitive data. The decision followed a series of incidents where popular software libraries were compromised due to weak or absent MFA protections.[1]

GitHub's approach involved extensive communication and education efforts to ensure a smooth transition for users. The platform provided detailed guidelines and support to assist users in setting up MFA, along with deadlines to ensure timely compliance. The result was a significant enhancement in the security of both individual projects and the wider open-source ecosystem hosted on GitHub.

Update Software on a Regular Basis

Outdated software can serve as a vulnerable target for cybercriminals, with unpatched systems often presenting the easiest entry points for malicious activities. By consistently updating software, organizations can patch known vulnerabilities and reduce the risk of a breach.

Keeping software up-to-date is not just about accessing new features; it is a necessary security practice that addresses vulnerabilities, such as security holes, and protects data from emerging threats. Regular updates are thus essential for securing applications, operating systems and even firmware from being compromised.

Patch Management

Patch management requires a systematic approach to all systems within an organization. This process includes several steps:

Identification of necessary updates: Regularly review updates released by software vendors to determine which patches are relevant to your systems;

Testing patches: Before broadly rolling out an update, it is advisable to test patches in a controlled environment. This step helps ensure that the updates do not cause issues within the existing system configurations;

Scheduled deployment: Plan and schedule updates to minimize disruption to business operations. This often involves deploying patches during off-peak hours; and

Verification: After updates are made, perform checks to ensure that patches have been applied successfully and that no unintended consequences affect system stability or security.

Automated Updates

Wherever possible, automating the update process can provide significant advantages. Automated systems can be set to scan for updates and download and apply them as soon as they are released by the software manufacturer. This ensures that systems are not left vulnerable for long periods of time, which can happen due to delays in manual update processes. Automation also reduces the workload on IT staff and minimizes human error that could result in missed updates or incorrect patch applications.

The SolarWinds Orion Security Breach

In late 2020, a sophisticated and far-reaching cyberattack was discovered. It involved the SolarWinds Orion platform, a widely used network management tool. This incident, often referred to as the Sunburst hack, affected numerous high-profile organizations, including U.S. government agencies and major corporations worldwide.

The breach was primarily executed through a supply chain attack, where malicious code was inserted into the software updates of the SolarWinds Orion platform. This malicious code created a backdoor into the networks of users who updated their SolarWinds software between March and June 2020. The attackers used this backdoor to infiltrate network traffic and steal data over several months without detection. [2]

The vulnerability was not in the original software but introduced through updates that were compromised. This highlights a significant risk in the software supply chain where even trusted updates can become vectors for cybersecurity threats. The attackers were able to circumvent traditional security measures by exploiting the trust relationship between software providers and their customers.

The detection of the SolarWinds breach led to an industry-wide reassessment of security practices around software updates and patch management. SolarWinds and affected organizations quickly worked to isolate compromised systems, remove malicious components and cut off attacker access. Following the breach, SolarWinds increased its focus on enhancing its software development environment. It implemented more rigorous security measures for its software development and distribution processes, including improved code auditing, enhanced monitoring of network and system activity, and more stringent controls over its build-and-release procedures.

The SolarWinds incident underscores the importance of not only keeping software up-to-date but also ensuring the security of the update processes themselves. Organizations must apply patches promptly to mitigate identified vulnerabilities. However, they also need to verify the integrity of patches and updates, especially those received from third-party vendors. Enhanced vigilance, including regular security assessments of vendors and their development environments, along with deploying endpoint detection and response tools, can help detect and mitigate unauthorized alterations to software.

Firewalls and Intrusion Detection Systems

Firewalls and Intrusion Detection Systems (IDS) are fundamental components of a cybersecurity strategy. These tools monitor and control incoming and outgoing traffic based on predefined security policies. Firewalls serve as the first line of defense in network security. They act as barriers between secure internal networks and potentially unsecure external networks, such as the Internet. A firewall examines all messages entering or leaving the internal network and blocks those that do not meet the specified security criteria.

Firewalls must be configured to deny all traffic by default and only allow traffic that is explicitly permitted. This setup minimizes potential entry points for attackers. It is also vital to configure firewall rules that are specific to the needs of the organization, such as blocking or allowing certain ports and protocols depending on the business operations.

Moreover, the configuration should be reviewed and updated regularly to adapt to new threats and to changes in the network environment. For example, as companies adopt new technologies or expand their network infrastructure, their firewall configurations may need to be adjusted to cover new potential vulnerabilities.

While firewalls control access to networks, Intrusion Detection Systems monitor network traffic to detect potential security breaches or malicious activities. IDS systems can be signature-based, meaning that they can detect known patterns of malicious activity, or they can be anomaly-based, meaning that they compare network activities to a baseline to detect unusual patterns that may indicate an attack.

Conduct Regular Monitoring and Testing

The effectiveness of firewalls and IDS often depends on continuous monitoring and regular maintenance. Security teams should monitor logs generated by these devices to detect any suspicious activity that could indicate a potential breach. Regularly updating and testing the configurations of firewalls and IDS are also necessary to ensure they are capable of defending against the latest types of cyber threats.

Implementing and maintaining firewalls and IDS with current configurations and regular monitoring as part of a broader security strategy significantly enhances an organization's ability to detect and respond to cyber threats. The case of the University of Giessen highlights the necessity of continuous improvement and vigilance in network security practices to safeguard against evolving cyber threats.

In 2019, Justus Liebig University Giessen in Germany faced a severe IT security incident that forced it to shut down its entire IT infrastructure. The attack was significant enough that the university had to register all staff and students anew with more stringent security protocols.[3] Post-incident analysis revealed that outdated firewall configurations and inadequate monitoring of network traffic were partly to blame. In response, the university overhauled its network security systems by implementing state-of-the-art firewalls and IDS with updated configurations tailored to the specific needs of their extensive network. The university also introduced regular audits and drills to test the systems' effectiveness and the staff's readiness to respond to further incidents.

Data Encryption

Data encryption is a vital security measure that converts sensitive data into a coded format, ensuring it remains inaccessible to unauthorized users. It protects data both at rest and in transit. This section describes the specifics of end-to-end encryption and the role of effective key management in maintaining secure information systems.

End-to-End Encryption

End-to-end encryption (E2EE) is designed to prevent data from being read or secretly altered, except by the true sender and recipient. The Data is encrypted on the sender's system or device, and only the recipient is able to decrypt it. Nobody in between, not even the service provider or Internet carrier, can read the data or tamper with it. This level of security is particularly crucial in the financial services, healthcare and legal sectors, where privacy and data security are governed by strict regulatory standards.

E2EE is not just about safeguarding data from external threats but also about minimizing the risk of internal threats. By ensuring that Data is encrypted from the point of origin to the point of destination, organizations can protect sensitive information against potential leaks and breaches that can occur during transmission.

The security of encrypted data is highly dependent on the effective management of **encryption keys**. Key management involves handling cryptographic keys in a secure manner throughout their lifecycle, including their creation, use, storage and eventual retirement or deletion. Here are the main aspects of key management:

> **Key Generation**: Secure and random key generation is essential to prevent predictable keys, which could be easily guessed by attackers;

Key Storage: Keys must be stored securely, using hardware security modules (HSMs) or encrypted databases to prevent unauthorized access;

Key Access: Strict controls should be implemented to ensure that only authorized personnel have access to encryption keys, minimizing the risk of insider threats; and

Key Rotation: Regularly updating or rotating encryption keys enhances security by limiting the amount of data that can be compromised in a single key exposure.

Organizations that neglect encrypting data or managing encryption keys are vulnerable to significant financial and reputational damage. The solution is to implement strong encryption practices and the secure management of encryption keys to protect sensitive information. The global hotel chain Marriott International is a case in point.
In 2018, Marriott announced that its reservation system had been hacked, leading to the exposure of personal information of approximately 500 million guests. The breach, which began in 2014, involved the Starwood reservations database. Investigations revealed that while the data were encrypted, the attackers had also accessed the encryption keys, which allowed them to decrypt the sensitive information.[4]

This incident underscores the necessity of not just encrypting data but also securely managing the encryption keys. Following the breach, Marriott took steps to enhance its encryption and key management practices. The company faced substantial fines for failing to adequately protect customer data.

Network Segmentation

Enhancing security through isolation network segmentation involves dividing a network into multiple segments or subnets, each acting as a separate security zone. This approach helps isolate systems and data, minimizing the potential impact of a breach by limiting an attacker's ability to move laterally across a network. This section explores how to effectively implement network segmentation, focusing on the identification of critical assets and the importance of regular audits to maintain network integrity.

The first step in implementing network segmentation is to identify which systems and Data is most critical to the organization's operations. This process involves a thorough assessment of the organization's resources to determine which assets, if compromised, would pose the most significant risk to the business continuity, legal compliance, trade secrets, and data security. Examples of critical assets might include systems that store sensitive customer information, financial records and proprietary intellectual property.

Once these critical assets are identified, they can be isolated from the broader network. This siloing helps protect them from unauthorized access and potential threats originating from less secure parts of the network. By doing so, organizations not only enhance the security of these vital assets but also ensure that, in the event of an attack, the damage is contained within a limited segment.

Network Segmentation and Implementation

Implementing network segmentation typically involves creating physical or virtual subnetworks that are separated by firewalls or other security controls. Each segment can have its own unique security policies tailored to the specific needs and risk levels of the assets it contains. For instance, a segment housing sensitive financial data may require stricter access controls and more robust monitoring systems than a segment used for guest Wi-Fi access.

To ensure that network segmentation remains effective, it is essential to conduct regular audits of the network segments to maintain their integrity. These audits should review how well the segmentation aligns with the organization's changing needs and whether it adheres to security best practices. Audits can identify any misconfigurations or oversights that may have occurred over time, allowing for timely adjustments to the network architecture. Regular audits also help verify that the security measures in place for each segment are functioning correctly and that no unauthorized pathways have been established between segments.

Sony Pictures

Following a high-profile breach in 2014, Sony Pictures Entertainment took significant steps to overhaul its network security, including implementing extensive network segmentation. The breach had exposed vast amounts of sensitive data, highlighting severe vulnerabilities in Sony's network security practices. In response, Sony identified systems and data that needed heightened protection and isolated these into separate network segments with enhanced security controls.

The post-breach network segmentation was part of a broader initiative to rebuild trust and reinforce Sony's defense mechanisms against future attacks. This effort resulted in technological improvements and a company-wide cultural shift towards greater security awareness and compliance.[5]

Endpoint Security: Safeguarding End-User Devices

Devices such as desktops, laptops, mobile devices and other network-connected devices often serve as entry points for cyberattacks and, if not properly secured, can significantly compromise an organization's entire network.

One of the first lines of defense in protecting endpoints is the installation and regular updating of antivirus and antimalware software. These tools are crucial for detecting, quarantining and removing malicious software that might infect devices. To ensure effectiveness, it is essential that these solutions are kept up-to-date with the latest virus definitions and scanning technology.

Regular updates help these tools keep pace with the evolving threat landscape, enabling them to effectively counter new and emerging malware. Beyond regular updates, it's important for organizations to conduct periodic scans and real-time monitoring of endpoints to detect threats before they can do significant damage.

Device Management Policies

Effective endpoint security also requires device management policies that control how devices are used and ensure they are secure, even if they become lost or stolen. Key aspects of device management include:

Password Requirements: Enforce password policies that require the use of complex passwords and regular password changes. This minimizes the risk of unauthorized access due to compromised credentials;

Software Restrictions: Limit the installation of unauthorized software on company devices to prevent employees from inadvertently installing malicious or unsecured applications that could pose security risks; and

Remote Wipe Capabilities: Implement systems that allow for the remote wiping of data on devices that are reported lost or stolen. This capability is crucial for protecting sensitive information in the event that a device cannot be recovered.

Effective endpoint security is a multi-faceted approach that requires both technological solutions and strategic policies. Organizations must equip their endpoints with the latest antivirus and antimalware software, enforce stringent device management policies, and foster a culture of security awareness among employees.

The Maersk Notpetya Attack

In chapter four, we drew your attention to how the global shipping giant Maersk was hit by the NotPetya malware in 2017. The attack disrupted operations worldwide and resulted in substantial financial losses, estimated at around US$300 million. NotPetya initially spread through a compromised update of Ukrainian tax software, subsequently infiltrating networks through vulnerabilities in unsecured endpoints.

In response to the attack, Maersk revamped its endpoint security measures. The company accelerated the deployment of advanced antivirus solutions across all endpoints and implemented stricter device management policies. Additionally, Maersk invested in educational programs to increase employee awareness about the risks associated with cyber threats and the importance of adhering to security practices.[6]

* * *

We have explored a range of strategies from data encryption and network segmentation to enhancing endpoint security. These measures are essential for establishing a secure and resilient infrastructure that protects against cyber threats. The efficacy of these measures requires regular audits and assessments. The next chapter illustrates how periodic evaluations can verify the effectiveness of security measures, identify areas for improvement, and ensure that cybersecurity strategies remain dynamic and adaptable in the face of evolving threats.

Endnotes

1 "Configuring two-factor authentication," GitHub Docs, https://docs. github.com/en/authentication/ securing-your-account-with-twofactor-authentication-2fa/configuring-two-factor-authentication.

2 "The SolarWinds hack timeline: Who knew what, and when?", https:// www.csoonline.com.

3 "Thousands of students in Germany queue for email access," BBC, 18 December 2019, https://www.bbc.com/news/technology-50838673.

4 "Marriott data breach FAQ: How did it happen and what was the impact?", CSO Online, https://www. csoonline.com/article/567795/marriottdata-breach-faq-how-did-it-happen-and-what-was-the-impact.html.

5 "The Sony Pictures Hack: Two Years Later," Technology and Operations Management (harvard.edu), https://d3.harvard.edu/platformrctom/submission/the-sony-pictures-hack-two-years-later/.

6 "Ransomware: The key lesson Maersk learned from battling the NotPetya attack," https://www.zdnet.com/article/ransomware-the-key-lesson-maersk-learned-from-battlingthe-notpetya-attack/.

CHAPTER 7

THE IMPORTANCE OF REGULAR AUDITS IN CYBERSECURITY MEASURES

Cybersecurity audits provide a structured method to evaluate an organization's security posture. They ensure that these defenses are effective against current threats and compliant with regulatory standards. This chapter addresses the significance of cybersecurity audits, the benefits they offer and the best practices for their execution.

Cybersecurity Audits: Rationale and Benefits

Regular audits are required for several reasons; they:

Identify Vulnerabilities: Audits systematically assess an organization's defenses to pinpoint vulnerabilities that could be exploited by cyber attackers;

Ensure Regulatory Compliance: Many industries are subject to specific cybersecurity regulations. Regular audits help ensure that organizations meet these requirements, thus avoiding potential legal penalties; and

Reveal Gaps in Cybersecurity Strategies: Through gap analysis, audits can highlight areas within the cybersecurity strategy that need strengthening or adjustment. This analysis helps organizations prioritize their security efforts effectively.

The benefits of conducting regular audits are numerous and include:

Proactive Threat Identification: Regularly scheduled audits help organizations identify and mitigate risks before they can be exploited;

Enhanced Security Posture: Continuous improvement of security measures keeps an organization ahead of potential threats; and

Increased Stakeholder Confidence: Demonstrating a commitment to stringent security measures enhances trust among customers, investors and partners.

To maximize the effectiveness of cybersecurity audits, organizations should adhere to several best practices, which include the following:

Use of Standardized Frameworks: Implementing recognized frameworks (such as ISO/IEC 27001, 116 NIST, or COBIT) provides a structured approach to the audit process;

Regular Scheduling: Audits should be conducted at regular intervals and in response to significant changes in the organization's network or operations; and

Involvement of Third Parties: Engaging independent third-party experts to conduct audits can provide an unbiased view of the cybersecurity posture.

Regular audits and assessments ensure that an organization's security measures are effective in protecting the organization against both current and emerging threats, ensuring their operations remain secure and resilient.

The Target Corporation Post-Breach Audit

Following the 2013 Target Corporation breach, the company undertook a comprehensive reassessment of its cybersecurity strategies. The breach, which affected millions of customers, exposed concerning vulnerabilities in Target's security measures. In response, Target conducted extensive internal and third-party audits that led to a major overhaul of its cybersecurity protocols. These audits identified where patching solutions were implemented and informed Target's approach to restructuring its digital security measures, including enhanced monitoring systems, improved endpoint protection and upgraded network segmentation.[1]

Types of Cybersecurity Audits

Cybersecurity audits are not one-size-fits-all; different types of audits serve various purposes, each in its own way contributing to a comprehensive cybersecurity strategy. Understanding the nuances of each type is essential for organizations aiming to protect themselves effectively against cyber threats. Three primary types of cybersecurity audits are up for discussion: (1) vulnerability assessments; (2) penetration testing, and (3) compliance audits.

1. Vulnerability Assessments

Vulnerability assessments can discover weaknesses within an organization's IT infrastructure that could be exploited by cybercriminals. The process involves scanning systems, networks and software applications to detect security issues. By identifying these weak points, organizations can prioritize their remediation efforts to strengthen their defenses before attackers can exploit these vulnerabilities.

The key components of vulnerability assessments include:

Automated Scanning: Using automated tools to scan for vulnerabilities across all systems;

Manual Review: Supplementing automated scans with manual reviews to explore deeper into the system's security setup; and

Risk Analysis: Evaluating the identified vulnerabilities to determine their potential impact and the risk they pose to the organization.

2. Penetration Testing

Penetration testing is often referred to as "ethical hacking," and involves simulating cyberattacks to evaluate the strength of an organization's defenses. Unlike vulnerability assessments, which only identify potential vulnerabilities, penetration tests actively seek weaknesses in an organization's cybersecurity measures and demonstrate where and how criminals can cripple an organization. A penetration test typically follows these steps:

Planning and Reconnaissance: Defining the scope of the test and gathering information about the target systems;

Scanning and Exploitation: Actively scanning and attempting to exploit identified vulnerabilities to gain unauthorized access;

Access and Movement: Exploring how deep into the network the penetration tester can navigate once access is gained; and

Analysis and Reporting: Providing detailed feedback on the vulnerabilities exploited, data accessed and recommendations for remediation.

3. Compliance Audits

Compliance audits are meant to ensure that an organization is adhering to legal, regulatory and technical standards. For instance, organizations handling personal data within the European Union must comply with General Data Protection Regulation (GDPR), while those involved with credit card processing need to adhere to Payment Card Industry Data Security Standard (PCI DSS). These audits assess whether an organization's security protocols meet the specific requirements set out by these regulations and standards.

Each type of cybersecurity audit—vulnerability assessments, penetration testing and compliance audits—plays a vital role in a comprehensive security strategy. By regularly conducting these audits, organizations can ensure they not only meet regulatory requirements but also maintain a robust defense against evolving cyber threats.

The New York Power Authority's Compliance Audit

The New York Power Authority (NYPA) undertook a comprehensive compliance audit to assess its adherence to NERC CIP standards—a set of requirements aimed at securing North America's power grid. The audit revealed several compliance discrepancies that could potentially impact the security and reliability of the power grid.[2]

Following the audit, NYPA implemented a series of measures to address these gaps, such as enhancing its security infrastructure, updating policies and increasing staff training on compliance issues. This comprehensive response not only aligned NYPA with NERC CIP standards, but also strengthened the company's overall security posture.

Cybersecurity Audits: A Systematic Approach

A systematic approach to conducting cybersecurity audits ensures comprehensive coverage and yields actionable insights that can significantly strength a company's defenses. This section covers preparing, executing and reporting on a cybersecurity audit, and emphasizes best practices for each phase.

1. Preparing for a Cybersecurity Audit

The first step in conducting an audit is thorough preparation. This phase involves defining the scope of the audit, which ensures that all necessary systems, networks and processes are included.

Preparation also involves gathering all relevant documentation, such as network diagrams, previous audit reports and security policies. Additionally, it's essential to ensure that all necessary permissions are in place to access the systems and information needed for the audit. This groundwork helps in setting clear expectations and facilitates a smooth audit process.

2. The Execution of a Cybersecurity Audit

The execution of an audit varies based on the type of audit being conducted, but generally includes a combination of automated scans, manual testing and interviews with staff. Automated scans can quickly identify known vulnerabilities across a wide array of systems and applications.

Manual testing, on the other hand, involves a deeper dive into specific areas, often carried out by skilled auditors who can identify issues that automated tools might miss. Interviews with staff are also crucial as they can reveal discrepancies between written policies and actual practices, as well as provide insights into potential areas of improvement that are not evident from system data alone.

During execution, it's vital that the audit is thorough and adheres to the predefined scope to ensure that all areas of potential risk are assessed and that the audit provides a true reflection of the organization's cybersecurity health.

3. Reporting

After the audit is completed, the next step is reporting. The audit report should compile all findings into a comprehensive document that highlights key vulnerabilities, assesses potential risks and provides clear recommendations for improvement. A well-documented report serves as a blueprint for addressing identified issues and tracking the progress of remediation efforts.

Anthem's Post-Audit Actions

Following a massive data breach in 2015 that affected nearly 80 million customers, Anthem Inc., a major health insurance company, undertook a rigorous audit process to identify the failures that led to the breach. The audit revealed significant gaps in the company's data security practices, including issues with user access controls and network encryption. Based on the audit findings, Anthem implemented a series of security measures, such as enhancing its identity and access management systems, upgrading data encryption techniques, and increasing the frequency of internal security audits. These changes not only improved Anthem's security infrastructure, but also restored trust with its customers and stakeholders.[3]

Anthem's example underscores the roles a detailed audit process and comprehensive reporting in recovering from a cybersecurity incident. A systematic approach to conducting cybersecurity audits is essential for uncovering vulnerabilities and enhancing security measures within an organization. By meticulously preparing, executing and reporting on audits, organizations can ensure that their cybersecurity strategies are both effective and aligned with best practices, ultimately safeguarding their digital assets against emerging threats.

Post-Audit: Turning Insights into Action

The true value of a cybersecurity audit lies not just in the identification of vulnerabilities and gaps but in the swift and effective actions taken to address these issues. The reason is that unresolved vulnerabilities can lead to severe security breaches. This section explores the steps necessary for prioritizing and remediating identified vulnerabilities, as well as reviewing remediation efforts to ensure their effectiveness.

Prioritization of Vulnerabilities

Once an audit is complete and vulnerabilities are identified, the next step is prioritization. Not all vulnerabilities pose the same level of risk to an organization; thus, it is essential to prioritize them based on their potential impact on the organization and the likelihood of exploitation by attackers. Factors to consider in this prioritization include the sensitivity of the affected data, the vulnerability's accessibility to potential attackers, and understanding the current threat landscape. This prioritization helps organizations allocate resources effectively, focusing on mitigating the most critical vulnerabilities first to reduce the overall risk.

Addressing and remediating the vulnerabilities identified in an audit is a multifaceted process that typically involves various actions depending on the nature of the vulnerabilities. Common remediation efforts include:

Patching Software: Applying patches to software and systems to fix known vulnerabilities;

Updating Protocols: Revising security protocols and infrastructure configurations to enhance security measures; and

Training Staff: Conducting targeted training sessions to address specific security weaknesses identified during the audit, particularly if the issues are related to user behavior or lack of awareness.

Effective remediation requires not just technical solutions but often a change in organizational processes and behaviors. Ensuring that all stakeholders understands their role in these remediation efforts—especially the leadership of an organization—is vital for successful implementation.

After remediation actions have been implemented, it is essential to review and verify that the vulnerabilities have been effectively addressed. This review process should involve retesting the remediated areas to ensure that the fixes are functioning as intended and that no new issues have been introduced during the remediation process. This important step closes the audit cycle and provides assurance that the organization's security posture has been enhanced. The University of York provides an instructive case study in effective post-audit action.

After suffering a significant phishing attack that compromised several student accounts, the university conducted a thorough audit that revealed vulnerabilities in its email system and user awareness. In response, the university prioritized these vulnerabilities based on the risk of potential data loss and disruption. The school promptly implemented enhanced email filtering technology, updated access control protocols and launched a comprehensive cybersecurity awareness program for students and staff.[4]

Following these remediation efforts, the university conducted a series of follow-up assessments to ensure that the measures were effective. These reviews confirmed that the new systems and protocols had significantly reduced the incidence of phishing attacks and improved the overall cybersecurity awareness within the campus community.

Frequency of Audits

Regularly scheduled audits are foundational to an effective cybersecurity strategy. These audits should be conducted at consistent intervals—typically annually or bi-annually—depending on the organization's risk profile and the sensitivity of the data it handles. Scheduled audits help organizations ensure continuous compliance with industry regulations and standards, and they provide a recurring opportunity to assess the effectiveness of current cybersecurity measures.

Scheduled audits typically involve a comprehensive review of the entire IT infrastructure, policies and practices. They are planned well in advance and are often aligned with the organization's fiscal calendar, allowing for systematic preparation and resource allocation. These audits assess various components of cybersecurity, including network security, physical security, access controls and data management practices, making sure that all aspects are up-to-date and effective.

While regular audits are essential, ad-hoc audits are equally important as they allow organizations to respond to specific events or changes that could potentially impact their security posture. These might include the introduction of new technology or systems, significant updates or changes in relevant legislation, or the occurrence of major global cyber incidents.

Ad-hoc audits provide the flexibility to address and assess risks introduced by sudden changes in the operational or threat landscape. For example, if an organization adopts a new cloud computing solution, an ad-hoc audit can specifically evaluate the security measures of this new system to ensure it integrates securely with existing infrastructure.

Adobe Systems Increases Auditing Frequency

Known for its extensive suite of software products, Adobe has frequently been the target of cyberattacks, primarily due to the widespread use of its software. Following a significant breach in 2013 that compromised millions of user accounts, Adobe enhanced its auditing frequency, incorporating both scheduled and ad-hoc audits into its cybersecurity regime. Adobe's approach includes routine audits of its software development and distribution processes, coupled with additional audits whenever new software versions are released or when significant vulnerabilities are discovered in existing products. This strategy allows Adobe to promptly address potential security flaws before they can be exploited by malicious actors.[5]

* * *

I cannot stress enough the importance of regular audits and assessments. These are essential practices to ensure the effectiveness of cybersecurity measures by keeping them up-to-date and responsive to the evolving digital landscape. Now we shift from proactive prevention to reactive strategies, focusing on managing the aftermath of a cyber breach. The next chapter describes effective management techniques and best practices to minimize damage, restore operations quickly, and maintain stakeholder trust, underscoring the critical importance of a well-prepared response plan in cybersecurity.

ENDNOTES

1   "Anatomy of the Target Data Breach: Missed Opportunities and Lessons Learned," ZDNET, https:// www.zdnet.com/article/anatomy-of-thetarget-data-breach-missed-opportunities-and-lessons-learned/.

2   "New York Power Authority: Selected Management and Operations Practices" (ny.gov), https:// www.osc.ny.gov/files/audits/2018- 01/sga-2016-15s20.pdf.

3   "$16 Million Anthem HIPAA Breach Settlement Takes OCR HIPAA Penalties Past $100 Million Mark," hipaajournal.com, and "Anthem Pays OCR $16 Million in Record HIPAA Settlement," HHS.gov, https:// www.hipaajournal.com/16-million-anthem-hipaa-breachsettlement-takes-ocr-hipaa-penalties-past-100-million-mark/.

4   "Report Phishing Email," Information Security at York (yorku.ca), https://infosec.yorku.ca/report-phishing-email/.

5   "Adobe's Approach to Managing Security Risk," updated April 2020, https://www.adobe.com/ca/ corporate-responsibility/data-security-risk.html.

CHAPTER 8

CRISIS MANAGEMENT: RESPONDING TO BREACHES

Cyber criminals are very sophisticated, and that puts all organizations at risk, even those that have prepared as best they can to deny a cyberattack. This chapter examines crisis management strategies with a focus on immediate steps an organization can take following detection of a cyber breach to mitigate operational impacts and potential reputational damage, and facilitate a structured recovery process.

When a Breach Is Detected

Swift and decisive action after detecting a breach can limit the damage and move the recovery trajectory forward. An effective immediate response entails:

Incident Isolation: The first step is to quickly isolate affected systems to prevent further spread of the breach. This may involve shutting down specific parts of the network, disabling access to certain applications, or segregating affected areas of the IT infrastructure. Rapid isolation helps contain the breach and reduces the risk of further infiltration or data loss.

Data Preservation: In parallel, all digital evidence related to the breach must be secured. This includes logs, system images and other relevant forensic data. Preserving this information is vital for analyzing the breach's origin, understanding how the breach occurred and identifying what data may have been compromised. Also, the may have applicability for legal and regulatory reasons.

Effective crisis management in cybersecurity hinges on the ability to respond swiftly and decisively to breaches. Organizations must have clear protocols for incident isolation and data preservation, ensuring they can stem the breach and gather necessary information for a thorough investigation. As demonstrated in the Equifax case, the subsequent steps, including detailed forensic analysis and transparent communication, are essential for mitigating damage, facilitating recovery and maintaining public trust.

In the 2017 Equifax data breach, the personal information of approximately 147 million people was exposed. In the immediate response phase, Equifax's actions were condemned because of delays in disclosure and perceived mismanagement. However, the lessons learned from this incident have informed better practices across the industry. Following the breach, Equifax implemented several emergency protocols, including the isolation of compromised systems and preservation of logs and other forensic data. Additionally, Equifax revamped its crisis management strategies to include faster public disclosure and more transparent communication strategies with stakeholders.

From this case, the broader industry learned the importance of having a predefined emergency response plan that includes not only technical responses but also comprehensive communication strategies. This ensures that all stakeholders, from employees to customers and regulators, are informed appropriately and in a timely manner, which is essential for maintaining trust and managing the fallout from the breach.

The Role of Communication in Crisis Management

A key crisis management protocol (among many we will discuss in this chapter) is an organization's communication strategy. Transparent and timely communication with both internal and external stakeholders can mitigate damage, manage public perception and ensure a coordinated recovery effort.

Internal Communication

The first step in crisis communication is to ensure that all employees within the organization are promptly informed about the breach. This communication should be clear and direct, outlining the nature of the breach and each team member's specific responsibilities in the response effort. Clear and effective internal communication will:

Reduce Panic: Properly informing employees helps to prevent panic and confusion, which obviously can exacerbate a crisis.

Better Coordinate the Response: When leaders help team members understand their roles and clarify the steps the organization is taking to address the breach, an organization-wide response will be better coordinated and reduce delays in implementing crisis management tools. Organizations should put in place communication protocols that include emergency contact lists, templates for initial notifications, and procedures for ongoing updates as more information becomes available.

External Communication

Once internal stakeholders are aligned, the focus shifts to external communication. This involves informing customers, partners and regulators about the breach. The key is to be honest and transparent about what has occurred and what is being done to resolve the issue. The goals of effective external communication are to:

Demonstrate Control: Assure stakeholders the situation is being managed and that measures are in place to secure systems and data.

Maintain Trust: Openness about the breach helps to maintain and even build trust by demonstrating the organization's commitment to transparency and accountability.

Meet Regulatory Requirements: Many jurisdictions require timely notification of data breaches, especially when sensitive information is involved. Compliance with these regulations will avoid legal repercussions and support responsible disclosure practices.

The T-Mobile Response to a Data Breach

In 2021, T-Mobile experienced a data breach affecting over 50 million individuals, including both current and past customers. The breached data included sensitive personal information. T-Mobile responded swiftly with a well-coordinated communication strategy. The company promptly informed affected individuals and regulatory bodies, outlining what data had been compromised and what steps were being taken to address the breach and prevent future occurrences.

T-Mobile's transparent approach included regular updates on its investigation and remediation efforts, as well as offering free identity protection services to affected customers. This proactive communication helped T-Mobile manage customer concerns and regulatory scrutiny, demonstrating the company's commitment to resolving the issue responsibly.[1]

Clear, transparent and timely communication during a cyber crisis goes a long way to managing stakeholder expectations and maintaining trust. Both internal and external communications must be handled carefully to ensure that everyone is accurately informed and coordinated in response efforts. As organizations continue to face cybersecurity threats, the ability to communicate effectively under pressure remains a vital aspect of crisis management, essential for navigating the challenges of a breach and leading the recovery process.

The Role of Investigation in Crisis Management

In the wake of a cybersecurity breach, conducting a thorough investigation is required for recovery and to mitigate the damage of future incidents. Two components of an investigation, forensic analysis and root cause analysis, help reveal the depth and impact of the breach, as well as the underlying vulnerabilities that allowed it to occur.

Forensic Analysis

The initial step in investigating a cyber incident is to perform a detailed forensic analysis. This process involves collecting and examining digital evidence to reconstruct the sequence of events leading up to, during and after the breach. The objectives of forensic analysis include:

Determining How the Breach Occurred: This involves identifying the methods and tools used by the attackers to gain unauthorized access.

Understanding What Data Were Affected: Assessing the scope of the data accessed, stolen or compromised is necessary for measuring the severity of the breach and for informing affected parties.

Identifying the Perpetrators: While it may not always be possible in the initial stages of a forensic analysis to attribute a breach to specific threat actors, when such actors are identified forensic analysis will provide insights into their motives and methods, which is useful for law enforcement and future security planning.

Forensic experts utilize a variety of tools and techniques to capture and analyze data from affected systems, ensuring that all evidence is preserved in a manner that maintains its integrity and admissibility in legal proceedings.

Root Cause Analysis

Following the forensic investigation, a root cause analysis is conducted to pinpoint the underlying reasons behind the breach. This analysis is necessary for developing effective remediation strategies that address not just the symptoms but the source of the problem. Root cause analysis typically explores several potential factors, including:

Technical Vulnerabilities: Were there flaws in the software or hardware that were exploited?

Human Error: Did the breach result from a mistake or oversight by an employee?

Policy Gaps: Were existing security policies inadequate or improperly enforced?

The Capital One Data Breach Investigation

A revealing example of a comprehensive investigation following a cybersecurity breach is the Capital One incident in 2019. Capital One suffered a significant data breach that affected approximately 100 million individuals in the United States. The breach was traced to a configuration vulnerability in a web application firewall.

A detailed forensic analysis revealed that a former Amazon Web Services (AWS) employee exploited a misconfigured web application to access the data stored on Capital One's servers. Following this discovery, Capital One conducted a root cause analysis that led to a broad reassessment of its cloud security practices. This incident highlighted the need for rigorous configuration management and ongoing security monitoring, especially in cloud environments.[2]

The investigation phase of crisis management, which involves the meticulous analysis of how a breach occurred and where the root causes lie, assists an organization in (1) understanding the broader security implications it is facing, and (2) implementing more rigorous security measures to mitigate future incidents.

Recovery: Navigating Post-Breach Restoration and Strengthening Defenses

Post-breach, the recovery process focuses on restoring affected systems and data, and fortifying defenses to prevent future incidents. The process is multi-faceted, involving data restoration from backups and the hardening of systems to address vulnerabilities exposed by the breach.

Data Restoration

The initial step organizations must take after a breach is to recover affected data from backups that were not compromised in the incident. Next, restored data must be meticulously scanned and cleaned to ensure there are no traces of malware or malicious entities that could reignite the breach. This involves (1) verifying the integrity of backup data; (2) ensuring that backups are comprehensive and up-to-date; and (3) utilizing clean recovery environments to prevent the reintroduction of threats.

System Hardening

Once data restoration is underway, attention must shift to hardening the systems to prevent a recurrence of similar breaches. This involves analyzing how the breach occurred and addressing the specific vulnerabilities that were exploited. System hardening measures include:

Patching Software: Applying the latest patches to fix vulnerabilities in software that were exploited by attackers.

Updating Protocols: Modifying security protocols and infrastructure configurations to enhance security measures and close gaps that were identified during the forensic investigation.

Reinforcing Network Defenses: Strengthening network defenses with additional security layers, such as enhanced firewall settings, intrusion prevention systems and more rigorous access controls.

The Sony PlayStation Network Recovery

To continue with the example of the breach of Sony's PlayStation Network in 2011, which affected millions of users worldwide, Sony took several steps to recover and enhance its security measures. Key recovery actions included shutting down the network temporarily to conduct a thorough security review, restoring services from backups that were confirmed to be secure, and hardening its systems against future attacks.

As part of the company's system hardening efforts, Sony enhanced its data protection practices, implemented a new data monitoring and management system, and increased encryption across its services. Sony also introduced a more robust authentication process for users to further secure user accounts. These measures were needed to restore service and user trust, and demonstrate the importance of comprehensive recovery strategies in the aftermath of a cybersecurity breach.

The recovery phase, when well-executed, can demonstrate that an organization can bounce back from a breach and emerge with a stronger cybersecurity posture and hopefully reduce the likelihood of similar future incidents.

Insights from Cybersecurity Incidents

Every cybersecurity crisis is an opportunity to learn. The post-crisis review offers valuable information an organization can use to become more resilient. The review process typically involves debriefing sessions and taking steps to update security protocols.

Debriefing Sessions

Debriefing sessions should involve key personnel who played a role in managing the crisis, from IT staff to senior management. The purpose of these sessions is to create an open forum for discussing what occurred, what was done to mitigate the breach, what went well, and, importantly, what could be improved. These discussions should cover:

The Effectiveness of the Response: This is an evaluation of the speed and efficacy of the response actions and the decision-making process that guided those actions.

Communication Efficiency: This is a review of how communication was handled internally and externally, including the timeliness and clarity of messages.

Role Performance: This is an assessment of how well each team and individual fulfilled their roles during the crisis.

Such post-review sessions help promote a culture of transparency and continuous improvement, as well as pinpointing specific areas where the crisis management strategy could be enhanced.

Updating Protocols

The insights gained from debriefing sessions are invaluable for updating existing protocols. Such updates may include making revisions to the organization's crisis management plans, cybersecurity defenses and response strategies. The key is to integrate the lessons learned into operational practices and training modules to ensure that the entire organization benefits from the new-found knowledge. Updates might involve:

Refining Detection Systems: Enhancing systems to detect similar threats more quickly or to catch breaches that previously went unnoticed.

Strengthening Defensive Measures: Adjusting firewalls, encryption methods and access controls based on the specifics of how the breach occurred.

Improving Training Programs: Updating training programs to include scenarios encountered during the incident to better prepare staff for future threats.

The Diginotar Post-Mortem Analysis

In 2011, DigiNotar, a Dutch certificate authority, suffered a breach that led to the issuance of fraudulent Secure Socket Layer (SSL) certificates. According to *Wired* magazine, the "breach allowed the intruder to trick DigiNotar's system into issuing him more than 500 fraudulent digital certificates for top internet companies like Google, Mozilla, and Skype. This meant that users who went to a supposedly secure page such as https://google.com were at risk of having a malicious third party who possessed the Google certificate pose as the legitimate site and trick the user into entering his username and password into the impostor site. The breach resulted in an immediate loss of trust in DigiNotar's integrity as an authority for issuing secure digital certificates, and resulted in swift action from the Dutch government, which pulled its business from the company."[3]

The breach had profound security implications, undermining trust in DigiNotar's services and leading to its bankruptcy. The post-mortem analysis revealed significant deficiencies in the company's security protocols and incident response. Importantly, the review highlighted a lack of adequate system segmentation and the absence of effective anomaly detection tools which could have mitigated the breach.

Following the incident, the broader cybersecurity community learned from DigiNotar's failure. Organizations worldwide began to place a greater emphasis on securing and monitoring their certificate issuance processes, implementing stricter controls, and improving transparency and response strategies.

The review and learning process following a cybersecurity incident can turn a negative event into an opportunity for growth and improvement. By thoroughly analyzing how a cybersecurity event happened, how it was handled, and how the aftermath was managed, organizations can ensure they are better prepared for future challenges, thereby enhancing their overall security posture and resilience.

* * *

As we conclude our exploration of effective crisis management, we have equipped ourselves with strategies to manage and mitigate the aftermath of cyber breaches effectively. By understanding the essential steps from immediate response through recovery and learning from each incident, organizations can strengthen their resilience against future cyber threats. In the next chapter the focus shifts to proactive strategies and ways to anticipate cybersecurity challenges and strategies to prepare to combat them effectively. By staying informed of the latest trends and advancements in cybersecurity and adapting their strategies accordingly, organizations can better safeguard their digital assets.

Endnotes

1 "The Cyberattack against T-Mobile and Our Customers: What happened, and what we are doing about it," T-Mobile Newsroom, https://www.t-mobile.com/news/network/cyberattack-against-tmobile-andour-customers.

2 "2019 Capital One Cyber Incident: What Happened?", Capital One https://www.capitalone.com/digital/ facts2019/.

3 "DigiNator Files for Bankruptcy in Wake of Devastating Hack," https//www.wired.com/2011/09/ diginator-hack/bankruptcy.

CHAPTER 9

FUTURE-PROOFING:
STAYING AHEAD OF EVOLVING THREATS

As you have come to realize in reading this book, cyber security needs to be steeped in an organization's culture. Cybersecurity is part strategy, part implementation, and part vigilance. It is an aspect of vigilance this chapter focuses on—continuous learning. If your organization has a learning culture, you will be able to ramp it up to remain current with cyber technology and the threat environment. If your organization needs to instill a learning culture, there is no time like the present. Continuous learning is a strategic approach to futureproofing an organization against evolving threats.

Aspects of Continuous Learning

The dynamic nature of cyber threats requires an equally dynamic approach to cybersecurity education and awareness. Encouraging a culture of continuous learning within an organization ensures that both leadership and staff remain knowledgeable about the latest threats, technological advancements and best practices in cybersecurity.

> **Training Programs**: Training programs must be conducted on a regular basis and for all employees. Remember that cybersecurity is not an "IT thing." As new threats emerge and technologies evolve, the content of training sessions must be updated to keep personnel aware of new threats. Ongoing training will ensure personnel are up to date with the latest security measures and how to implement them effectively. Bringing in external experts to conduct specialized training sessions can provide valuable insights from different perspectives and keep the training material fresh and relevant.

Cybersecurity Conferences: Attending leading cybersecurity conferences is another excellent way for key personnel to gain exposure to the latest ideas and developments in the field. These conferences provide a platform to learn from peer experiences, engage with experts, and explore new technologies and strategies that can be implemented to enhance the organization's cybersecurity posture.

IBM's Cybersecurity Training Initiative

A compelling example of an organization that has effectively implemented continuous learning is IBM. IBM invests heavily in ongoing education and training for its employees to help its people stay current with risks inherent in technologies used for cyber threats. One of the initiatives includes the IBM Cybersecurity Leadership University, a program specifically designed for its executives and managers.

This program covers the technical aspects of cybersecurity and focuses on the leadership capabilities and strategic thinking required to implement security initiatives successfully. Additionally, IBM encourages and sponsors its IT security staff to attend external conferences and workshops to refresh their knowledge.[1]

IBM's proactive approach to mitigating the impact of cyber threats places a great deal of emphasis on continuous learning. Organizations must stay ahead of potential security issues and have a plan in place to defend against attacks. Such a commitment to education and training fosters a knowledgeable workforce capable of responding to challenges in innovative and effective ways.

By keeping training programs updated and leading and attending conferences, organizations can better equip their people with the knowledge and skills needed to accelerate a strong resilience posture.

Investing in Research and Development: Catalyzing Cybersecurity Innovation

Hand-in-hand with continuous learning is an organization's commitment to investing in R&D. Organizations that invest in R&D are (1) better prepared to meet current security challenges, and (2) better positioned to anticipate and counteract emerging threats. We'll examine how investing in R&D enhances an organization's cybersecurity capabilities and strategic advantage.

Emerging Technologies

The rapid development of technologies such as artificial intelligence (AI) and quantum computing (QC) is reshaping the cybersecurity landscape. AI technologies are a powerful tool; they can identify and respond to threats by analyzing vast amounts of data for anomalous patterns that may indicate a security breach. For example, AI-driven security systems can automate complex processes for detecting, containing, and mitigating intrusions more efficiently than traditional methods.[2]

However, as these technologies evolve, they also introduce new challenges and vulnerabilities. For instance, quantum computing presents a potential risk to the encryption standards that currently protect vast amounts of sensitive data. Anticipating these changes, organizations can invest in quantum-resistant cryptography to safeguard against future threats that could exploit quantum technologies.

In-House Cyber Labs

Establishing dedicated cyber labs within an organization is another effective strategy for leveraging R&D in cybersecurity. These labs serve as hubs for innovation and experimentation, where new technologies can be tested and refined in a controlled environment. Activities in cyber labs include:

Technology Testing: New software, hardware and security protocols can be rigorously tested to assess their effectiveness and identify any potential vulnerabilities before those technologies are widely deployed.

Penetration Testing and Simulations: Cyber labs can conduct regular penetration tests and simulate cyberattack scenarios to evaluate the resilience of the organization's systems and networks.

Collaborative Research: These labs often collaborate with academic institutions, industry partners and government agencies, fostering a collaborative approach to cybersecurity challenges.

The Google X Cybersecurity Project

An example of R&D investment is Google's Project Zero, an in-house research unit dedicated to finding security vulnerabilities, known as "zero-day" vulnerabilities, across various software platforms and networks. The team consists of expert security analysts focused on discovering flaws that could be exploited by hackers.

Project Zero's work has been instrumental in enhancing the security of Google's own products and those developed by other major software companies. By responsibly disclosing vulnerabilities to the affected software vendors, Google has helped strengthen the security of widely used software products globally. This proactive approach both protects users and encourages the broader tech community to prioritize security in software development.[3]

By exploring emerging technologies and establishing in-house cyber labs, organizations enhance their security solutions and collectively contribute to the global cybersecurity ecosystem. This forward-thinking approach ensures that the organization is well-prepared to anticipate and tackle future cyber threats, thereby maintaining its competitive edge and safeguarding its critical assets.

Collaborate to Stay Ahead of Threats

Defending against cybersecurity challenges is immeasurably improved when organizations collaborate. Collaboration among organizations, industry groups and governmental bodies can significantly amplify an organization's defenses by pooling resources, knowledge and strategic insights. This section explores the essential role of collaboration in cybersecurity through information sharing and industry alliances.

Information Sharing

One of the most effective ways organizations can bolster their cybersecurity posture is by establishing robust channels for sharing information about potential threats, vulnerabilities and best practices. Information sharing involves exchanging valuable security insights with trusted partners, which can include other businesses, cybersecurity firms and government agencies. This collective pool of knowledge helps organizations stay abreast of the latest threats and defensive tactics, enhancing their ability to respond to attacks quickly and effectively.

Effective information sharing can be facilitated through:

Dedicated Communication Platforms: Implement secure platforms that allow for the rapid exchange of information among trusted entities.

Regular Meetings and Briefings: Schedule regular interactions among network members to discuss recent threats and developments in cybersecurity.

Joint Training Exercises: Conduct shared training sessions and cybersecurity drills to improve response capabilities across participating organizations.

Industry Alliances

Joining industry-specific alliances or groups focused on cybersecurity is another vital strategy for collaborative defense. These alliances are often comprised of companies that face similar threats and share common goals in protecting their sector's infrastructure. Participation in such groups can provide several benefits such as:

Access to Specialized Threat Intelligence: Members can receive tailored intelligence specific to their industry's unique threats.

Resource Pooling for Advanced Solutions: Alliances often develop solutions that might be too costly or complex for individual organizations to undertake alone.

Collective Advocacy: Groups can work together to influence policy and regulatory developments that benefit the broader industry.

The Financial Services Information Sharing and Analysis Center

An example of industry collaboration is the Financial Services Information Sharing and Analysis Center (FS-ISAC). Established in 1999 in response to Presidential Directive 63, FS-ISAC is a nonprofit organization that facilitates information sharing among financial institutions globally to combat cyber threats. Members include banks, credit unions, payment processors and investment firms, among others.

FS-ISAC provides a platform for its members to share real-time intelligence on threats, vulnerabilities and remedies. It also coordinates closely with governmental agencies to provide its members with timely notifications and advisory services. This collaborative effort has been instrumental in thwarting numerous cyber threats and has established FS-ISAC as a model for sector-specific cybersecurity alliances.[4]

In the battle against cyber threats, the benefits of collaboration are clear. By sharing information and resources, and by joining industry-specific alliances, organizations can improve their cybersecurity capabilities. These collaborative efforts improve individual organizational security and strengthen the overall security posture of entire sectors and industries, making them less vulnerable to attacks.

Proactive Defense: Staying Ahead of Cyber Threats

Rather than reacting to incidents as they occur, a proactive approach involves continuously searching for and addressing potential security gaps before they can be exploited by attackers. Implementing a proactive defense includes red teaming and threat hunting, which help organizations anticipate and neutralize threats before they result in damage.

Red Teaming

As discussed in chapter five, red teaming is an exercise in proactive defense. It involves the use of external experts to simulate realistic cyberattacks on an organization's systems. These simulations are designed to mimic the tactics, techniques and procedures used by actual attackers, providing a rigorous test of all aspects of an organization's cybersecurity protocols. Red team exercises help identify vulnerabilities in both infrastructure and response strategies, offering valuable insights that can be used to strengthen security measures. Key aspects of red teaming include:

Regular Engagements: Conducting red team exercises on a regular basis ensures that defenses are continuously evaluated and improved.

Realistic Scenarios: Simulations should reflect the most likely and damaging types of attacks the organization might face, based on current threat intelligence.

Integrated Responses: Red teaming must include the IT security team and other relevant departments such as communications and human resources to ensure a holistic response to incidents.

Threat Hunting

Threat hunting goes beyond traditional monitoring and detection by actively searching for malicious activity that has evaded existing security measures. This proactive technique involves analysts and cybersecurity professionals using their knowledge of the latest cyber threats to hypothesize where attackers might be hiding or what tactics they might use next. The goal is to identify and mitigate threats before they manifest into full-blown breaches. Threat hunting involves:

Hypothesis-Driven Investigations: Starting from hypotheses based on recent cyber threats or anomalies observed in the system.

Using Advanced Tools: Leveraging sophisticated cybersecurity tools to sift through network and application logs, as well as other data sources, to detect hidden threats.

Continuous Learning: Regularly updating the threat hunting strategies based on new information and tactics observed in the industry.

Lockheed Martin

Lockheed Martin, the global aerospace, defense and security company, implemented an advanced proactive defense strategy known as the Cyber Kill Chain, which breaks down the stages of a cyberattack and develops specific defenses for each stage. Part of this strategy involves regular red teaming and sophisticated threat hunting activities, which have allowed Lockheed Martin to stay ahead of potential cyber threats. The company's proactive stance has resulted in safeguarding critical defense information and positioning the company as a leader in cybersecurity practices within the defense industry.

Proactive defense is essential for modern organizations to effectively anticipate and counteract cyber threats. By integrating practices like red teaming and threat hunting into their cybersecurity strategies, organizations can detect vulnerabilities early, respond quickly and maintain a strong security posture.

Scenario Planning: Preparing for Future Cybersecurity Challenges

Scenario planning helps organizations prepare for a range of potential threats and outcomes. This approach involves crafting possible scenarios that could impact cybersecurity and developing plans to address events should they occur. Scenario planning includes cyber drills and future threat analysis.

Cyber Drills

One of the most effective ways to prepare for potential cybersecurity incidents is through conducting cyber drills. These exercises simulate various cyberattack scenarios to test an organization's readiness and the effectiveness of its response protocols. Cyber drills help identify vulnerabilities in both technical defenses and human responses, and provide valuable insights into how security measures perform under stress. Key aspects of effective cyber drills include:

Realistic Simulations: Creating scenarios that are based on realistic and plausible threats, which could involve anything from a ransomware attack to a full-scale data breach.

Involvement of All Relevant Parties: Ensuring that not just the IT department but all relevant areas of the organization participate, including legal, communications and executive leadership.

After-Action Reviews: Conducting thorough debriefings after each drill to discuss what went well and what could be improved, leading to actionable insights for enhancing future responses.

Future Threat Analysis

In addition to preparing for immediate and known threats, future threat analysis involves looking ahead to anticipate new risks that could emerge from changes in technology, geopolitical shifts or new industry practices. This proactive approach involves:

Engaging Experts: Utilizing cybersecurity experts who can analyze trends in technology and cybercrime to predict how new threats might develop.

Industry Collaboration: Participating in industry groups and forums to share insights and gather intelligence on emerging threats and vulnerabilities.

Continuous Learning: Keeping up-to-date with the latest research and developments in cybersecurity to ensure that the organization's defenses evolve as new threats emerge.

The Zurich Insurance Cyber Scenario Planning

Zurich Insurance is an example of an organization that developed a comprehensive scenario planning process—one that includes regular cyber drills and extensive analysis of future cyber threats. These drills have enabled Zurich to test and improve its cybersecurity response strategies, and to understand potential impacts on its business operations.

Zurich's future threat analysis also involves collaboration with cybersecurity firms and other financial institutions to develop a deep understanding of the evolving risk landscape. This ongoing analysis allows Zurich to continuously update its cybersecurity strategies and policies to address both current and potential future threats effectively.

Scenario planning requires conducting cyber drills on a regular basis and engaging in future threat analysis, organizations can ensure they are well-prepared to handle a variety of cyber incidents. Thorough preparation increases the speed at which an organization can respond to a cyberattack and enables long-term resilience against evolving cybersecurity challenges. Through meticulous planning and proactive measures, organizations can safeguard their assets and maintain trust among their stakeholders in an increasingly uncertain digital world.

* * *

We have seen that continuous learning, innovation, collaboration with industry partners and scenario planning are tools organizations use to defend against current threats and adapt to new challenges.

Transitioning to the next chapter, we shift our focus to aspects of collaborating with external partners and vendors. Organizations increasingly rely on external partnerships to grow their business and, as we've seen, to improve their cybersecurity measures. How can we make sure that collaboration and interaction with third-party entities are secure? That's the topic we turn to next.

ENDNOTES

1 "IBM Impact Feature: Apprenticeship Program," IBM, https://www.ibm. com/impact/feature/ apprenticeship.

2 "MIT GE EPIC," April 2021, pdf, https://innovation.mit.edu/assets/MIT-GE-EPIC-final_April-2021_FINAL2. pdf 151.

3 "Google Establishes Asia-Pacific Cybersecurity Hub in Tokyo," Techopedia, https://www.techopedia. com/news/googleestablishes-asia-pacific-cybersecurity-hub-in-tokyo.

4 Financial Services Information Sharing and Analysis Center (fsisac.com), https://www.fsisac.com/.

Chapter 10

Collaborating with External Partners and Vendors

In a global digital economy, organizations rely on external partnerships and vendors for cloud computing services and specialized software solutions. While these collaborations deliver many advantages, they also pose cybersecurity risks such as breaches. Organizations must take steps to have proper oversight of third-party relationships to safeguard their intellectual property and assets.

Vetting Partners

For third-party relationships, a thorough vetting process must be undertaken to make sure of the security integrity of existing partners and to test the security integrity of potential vendors. This process involves several key steps:

Due Diligence: Thorough background checks are essential. These checks include a review of potential partners' cybersecurity policies, their history of cybersecurity incidents, and their reputation within the industry. This process helps determine whether the security standards of a vendor align with the organization's requirements.

On-site Visits: Conducting on-site visits can provide valuable insights into the operational protocols and security measures implemented by the partner. Observing a vendor's operations firsthand can reveal the dynamic aspects of its security protocols that might not be evident through an examination of its documents.

For emphasis, the goal of the vetting process is to discover any questions or concerns over a partner's cybersecurity measures, which may put the organization at risk.

Target's Vendor Security Enhancement

As you will recall, in 2013 Target Corporation suffered a huge data breach, which was traced back to a vulnerability introduced by an HVAC vendor. This incident exposed the payment information of millions of customers and highlighted the risks associated with third-party vendors.

In response, Target overhauled its vendor management policies, instituting a comprehensive vendor-risk management program. This program included stricter cybersecurity criteria for selecting and retaining vendors and a continuous monitoring strategy to ensure ongoing compliance with Target's security standards. The company also began conducting regular security assessments of its vendors and required them to undergo cybersecurity awareness training.[1] Through its proactive approach, Target fortified its defenses against potential threats from third-party vendors and restored trust with its customers and stakeholders.

For any organization, collaborating with external partners and vendors is table stakes in our digitally interconnected world, but it requires careful management to mitigate associated cybersecurity risks. By implementing thorough vetting processes, such as conducting due diligence and on-site visits, organizations can firm up their security protocols.

The case of Target is a powerful reminder of the potential consequences of neglecting third-party vendor security and the benefits of a rigorous vendor risk-management strategy. As businesses continue to integrate more deeply with external entities, it is essential that strict cybersecurity standards be maintained throughout the supply chain.

The Role of Regular Audits in Vetting

Establishing trust with external partners and vendors is a two-way street. And such trust requires taking steps to maintain it. Regular audits measure how well partners are adhering to agreed-upon security standards. We'll examine best practices for conducting these audits, including both scheduled and surprise checks, to guarantee that partner security measures remain robust and compliant.

Scheduled Audits

Scheduled audits are systematic reviews that should be integrated into the partnership agreement and conducted at regular intervals—typically annually or bi-annually. These audits allow an organization to assess and verify the ongoing cybersecurity practices of their partners and ensure that they are in line with the latest security standards and compliance requirements. The key elements of scheduled audits include:

Comprehensive Review: Such a review evaluates the partner's cybersecurity policies, procedures and infrastructure to ensure they meet the required standards.

Documentation Check: A document check examines the partner's record of security incidents, response strategies and updates to their security protocols.

Compliance Verification: A compliance verification assesses to what degree a partner is complying with relevant laws, regulations and industry standards, which may evolve over time.

Scheduled audits provide a regular, structured opportunity to assess risks and reinforce security expectations, fostering a continuous improvement environment.

Surprise Audits

In addition to the planned audits, surprise audits serve the purpose of discovering vulnerabilities in a partner's day-to-day operational security, because obviously a partner does not have time to prepare for the audit. Key benefits of surprise audits focus on:

Operational Transparency: Both parties gain insight into the actual daily practices and operational challenges faced by the partner.

Immediate Vulnerability Detection: Security gaps may be identified that require urgent attention, which might be overlooked during routine checks.

Enhanced Security Posture: The unplanned audit encourages partners to maintain constant vigilance and high standards of cybersecurity.

The Cisco Partner Security Program

Cisco manages the security regime of its partners with its auditing protocols. The company implemented a comprehensive partner security program that includes both scheduled and surprise audits. This program helps ensure that their partners, who often handle sensitive data and access Cisco's internal resources, maintain the highest levels of security compliance.

Cisco's program assesses compliance with technical standards as well as evaluating operational practices and a partner's ability to respond to diverse threats. The results from these audits have helped Cisco and its partners identify potential security improvements and have driven higher standards across their network, thereby reducing overall risk.[2]

Regular audits, both scheduled and surprise, are essential for maintaining a secure and trustworthy relationship with external partners and vendors. A rigorous auditing process can go a long way to help organizations and its partners and vendors protect themselves against potential breaches.

Clear Contracts: Establishing Cybersecurity Protocols through Legal Agreements

In the complex web of digital collaborations, clear legal agreements with external partners and vendors are required to define parties' cybersecurity responsibilities. Relationship management relies on clarity of accountabilities for compliance and incident handling, particularly when sensitive Data is involved. This section explores the critical aspects of data handling and incident reporting in the crafting of clear contracts.

Data Handling

Legal agreements must meticulously detail how all data exchanged or accessed by partners and vendors will be handled, stored and protected. Specific clauses should address several key areas:

Data Encryption: The contract should specify the encryption standards required for storing and transmitting data. This ensures that all sensitive information remains protected from unauthorized access during transit and at rest.

Backup Protocols: The contract should outline the methods and frequency of data backups. This ensures that all parties maintain copies of data that can be restored in the event of data loss or corruption.

Access Controls: The contract should clearly define who can access which data, and under what circumstances can step in to prevent unauthorized access and deal with data breaches. The contract should specify the roles and responsibilities of all parties regarding data access and the procedures for modifying these access rights.

By explicitly stating these protocols, organizations can ensure that data handling by partners aligns with their own security standards and compliance requirements.

Incident Reporting

Another vital component of cybersecurity contracts is the protocol for incident reporting. This section of the agreement should outline:

Reporting Timeframe: Establish a clear deadline for reporting cybersecurity incidents once they are discovered. This prompt reporting is crucial to mitigate the damage and begin the response and recovery process swiftly.

Details Required: Specify the type of information that must be reported about an incident. This often includes the nature of the breach, the type of data compromised, the suspected cause of the incident and the impact assessment.

Communication Channels: Designate specific points of contact and communication channels for incident reporting to ensure that information is quickly directed to the right personnel.

The Equifax Contractual Overhaul Post-Breach

Following the massive data breach in 2017, Equifax took significant steps to overhaul its approach to partner contracts, especially concerning data handling and incident reporting. Learning from the incident, Equifax implemented stringent contractual requirements with its partners, mandating higher security measures for data protection and specific protocols for incident reporting. According to *Wired* in a 2018 article, "Equifax reported that 'enhancing the experience of consumers who engage with us' is one of the four main priorities that have driven the company's transformation. Julia Houston, Equifax's chief transformation officer, a role created in October [2017] to coordinate breach remediation efforts, explains that the others include rebuilding trust with the bureau's actual customers, becoming an industry leader in data security, and investing in network security improvements."[3]

These revised contracts now include clauses that require partners to adopt advanced encryption methods, conduct regular security audits, and report any security incidents within twenty-four hours of discovery. These measures are designed to improve data protection and ensure the company is able to respond to and manage incidents more effectively, minimizing potential damage and restoring trust with customers and stakeholders.

The clearer the contract, the less room there is for parties to misconstrue their cybersecurity responsibilities. By explicitly addressing data handling and incident reporting requirements, organizations can create a resilient framework that maintains data integrity and provides a clear roadmap for managing cybersecurity incidents in an increasingly interconnected business environment.

Continuous Communication: Sustaining Security through Partnership

Organizations must maintain a continuous and open line of communication with external partners and vendors in order to ensure that all parties remain aligned in their efforts to safeguard sensitive information and infrastructure. Structured communication may include two necessary components: monthly review meetings and joint training sessions.

Monthly Review Meetings

Monthly review meetings serve as a structured platform for all parties involved to discuss and synchronize their cybersecurity strategies. These sessions are vital for:

Addressing Updates: Regularly reviewing any changes or updates in cybersecurity policies, tools and protocols ensures that all parties are on the same page and implementing the most effective strategies.

Identifying Challenges: Discussing ongoing or emerging cybersecurity challenges allows for a proactive approach to address potential vulnerabilities before they are exploited.

Resolving Concerns: These meetings provide a forum for airing and resolving any concerns regarding cybersecurity practices, and fostering trust and transparency between all involved parties.

The regular cadence of these meetings helps maintain a rhythm of accountability and ensures that both sides commit to their cybersecurity responsibilities. They also facilitate timely adaptations to new threats and changes in the digital landscape.

Collaborative Training Sessions

Joint training sessions with partners and vendors are another critical element of continuous communication. These sessions are beneficial for:

Unified Security Practices: Training together ensures that all parties understand and implement uniform security measures, reducing the risk of breaches due to inconsistent practices.

Knowledge Sharing: Collaborative training provides an opportunity for sharing insights about emerging cybersecurity threats and the latest defense technologies. This shared learning experience can elevate the overall security posture of all involved.

Strengthening Relationships: Regular interaction during training sessions helps build and maintain strong relationships, fostering a collaborative environment that is essential for effective cybersecurity.

Cisco's Partner Communication Strategy

A standout example of effective continuous communication in cybersecurity is Cisco's approach with its global network of partners. Cisco established a comprehensive communication strategy that includes regular monthly review meetings and collaborative training programs with its vendors and partners. These initiatives are designed to ensure that every entity within Cisco's ecosystem is not only aware of the best cybersecurity practices but also actively implements them.[4]

Cisco's strategy involves using a dedicated partner portal for sharing real-time security updates and threat intelligence. The company also hosts annual security conferences that bring together all its partners to discuss new challenges, share strategies and undergo joint training sessions. This proactive and inclusive approach has helped Cisco and its partners stay ahead of potential security threats and maintain a high standard of security across their operations.

Maintaining continuous communication with partners and vendors is essential for ensuring that cybersecurity measures are consistently applied and adapted. Through monthly review meetings and collaborative training sessions, organizations can build a more resilient and responsive security infrastructure. Cisco's example demonstrates how a well-structured communication strategy can enhance cybersecurity collaboration and lead to a stronger, more secure network.

Exit Strategy: Securing End-of-Collaboration Transitions

In the lifecycle of business collaborations, there often comes a time when partnerships need to be concluded or restructured. When these transitions occur, it's imperative to follow best practices for managing cybersecurity protocols to prevent any potential data breaches or security lapses. This section outlines the essential components of an effective exit strategy for cybersecurity, focusing on secure data transfer and access revocation.

Data Transfer and Deletion

A critical aspect of any exit strategy is the secure transfer or deletion of data at the end of a collaboration. This process should be clearly outlined in the initial agreements and executed with precision to ensure data integrity and security. Important considerations include:

Secure Data Transfer: If data need to be transferred back to the organization or to another party, it should be done using secure, encrypted channels to prevent interception. The transfer process should be documented and verified by both parties to ensure complete and accurate handover.

Data Deletion: Where data need to be deleted from a partner's systems, the deletion must be complete and irreversible. Employing methods such as cryptographic wiping or physical destruction of storage devices can prevent any possibility of data recovery.

Detailed protocols for these processes should be established and agreed upon at the start of any partnership to avoid complications at the end of the collaboration.

Revoking System Access

Another critical element of an exit strategy is the revocation of any access rights or credentials that were granted during the partnership. This step is vital to safeguard the organization's systems and data after the separation. Effective measures include:

Revoking Credentials: All credentials such as usernames, passwords and API keys should be immediately deactivated or changed. This prevents any residual access that could be exploited maliciously.

Securing Access Points: Beyond just revoking credentials, it's important to review and secure all access points that were available to the partner, including remote access services and third-party applications.

The IBM Cloud Transition Protocol

An illustration of a model exit strategy is IBM's approach during its transition phases with cloud service customers. IBM has established a comprehensive protocol for securely transitioning data and access rights at the end of cloud service agreements. This protocol involves secure data migration tools that ensure data integrity during transfer, followed by rigorous data deletion processes to cleanse any residual data from IBM's systems.

Moreover, IBM implements a systematic access revocation process that involves an audit of all access points and credentials issued during the collaboration. This ensures that no unauthorized access remains possible post-transition. IBM's thorough approach in these transitions showcases best practices in maintaining cybersecurity standards, even after the end of a collaboration.[5]

Having a clear exit strategy is essential for maintaining cybersecurity at the end of collaborations. By carefully managing data transfer and access rights, organizations can mitigate risks associated with the transition phases of partnerships. Effective planning and execution of these strategies ensure that all parties conclude their engagements securely, maintaining integrity and trust even as paths diverge.

* * *

As we wrap up our discussion on secure collaborations with external partners and vendors, we have highlighted the importance of communication, audits and clear legal agreements throughout the lifecycle of any partnership. Effective strategies for entering and exiting collaborations help ensure that both parties maintain strong cybersecurity postures.

Next, we shift our focus to compliance with laws and regulations that govern data security and privacy. Understanding these legal frameworks is essential for any organization to protect themselves from cyber threats and also navigate the potential legal ramifications of cybersecurity practices. Staying compliant is not just a legal obligation, but a strategic advantage in reinforcing trust and integrity in the digital age.

ENDNOTES

1   "Four Ways Target Dynamically Tracks the Most Alarming Threats," Cybersecurity Dive, https:// www.cybersecuritydive.com/news/target-threat-intelligence/634596/.

2   "Cisco Partner Program - Cisco," https://www.cisco.com/site/us/en/partners/cisco-partner-program/index.html Cisco - Insight Partner, https://solutions.insight.com/About/Partners/Cisco.

3   "Equifax's Security Overhaul, a Year after Its Epic Breach," *Wired magazine* (July 25, 2018), https://www.wired.com/story/equifax-security-overhaul-year-after-breach/.

4   "Partner Communication," Cisco Partner Marketing DG Guide (2017), https://www.cisco.com/c/dam/global/th_th/assets/partners/pdfs/cisco_partner_marketing_dg_guide_apj_for_q3fy17.pdf.

5   "IBM Cloud Transit Gateway," IBM, https://www.ibm.com/products/transit-gateway Getting started with IBM Cloud Transit Gateway , IBM Cloud Docs, https://cloud.ibm.com/docs/transit-gateway?topic= transit-gateway-getting-started&interface=ui.

CHAPTER 11

COMPLYING WITH GLOBAL CYBERSECURITY REGULATIONS

Governments and international bodies have implemented stringent regulations to safeguard data and ensure the security of the digital ecosystem. These regulations are continually updated in response to the increasing complexity of cyber threats. For business leaders, adherence to these regulations is both a legal obligation and vital aspect of maintaining stakeholder trust and demonstrating corporate responsibility. This section describes the regulatory environment and actions organizations must take to remain compliant.

Where and How Do Regulations Apply?

Cybersecurity regulations have international and domestic implications. Here are two examples:

General Data Protection Regulation (GDPR): Enacted by the European Union in 2018, GDPR is one of the most stringent privacy and security legal frameworks in the world. It imposes obligations onto organizations anywhere in the world that collect data on EU citizens. The regulation emphasizes transparency, security and accountability by organizations, making it necessary for organizations to have data protection and security measures in place which meet GDPR standards. GDPR has set a benchmark for privacy laws worldwide, which has galvanized governments of many countries to reevaluate and strengthen domestic laws and regulations.

California Consumer Privacy Act (CCPA): Enacted by the State of California, CCPA provides consumers with significant control over how businesses collect and use their personal information. Introduced in 2020, CCPA has prompted state governments and businesses across the United States to alter their practices to ensure compliance.

Marriott International and GDPR Compliance

An example of how a multi-national organization was affected by GDPR regulations is the hotel chain Marriott International. In 2018, Marriott disclosed a data breach of its Starwood brand that affected up to 500 million guests, with unauthorized access dating back to 2014. This breach included sensitive personal information such as names, phone numbers, email addresses, passport numbers and travel information. As the breach affected EU citizens, Marriott faced significant scrutiny under GDPR.

Following the breach, in 2020 the United Kingdom's Information Commissioner's Office (ICO) initially proposed a fine of approximately £99 million under GDPR regulations due to Marriott's inadequate due diligence during its acquisition of Starwood hotels and subsequent failures to secure its systems.[1] Marriott's experience underscores the importance of GDPR compliance and demonstrates the potential financial and reputational impacts of non-compliance.

Strategies for Effective Compliance

For businesses to navigate this complex regulatory landscape effectively, several strategies can be employed:

Regular Compliance Audits: Regular audits help ensure that business practices remain in compliance with applicable laws, especially as regulations evolve.

Dedicated Compliance Teams: Establishing specialized compliance teams can help businesses stay current on legal requirements and implement necessary changes promptly.

Ongoing Education: Regular training sessions for employees on compliance issues demonstrates the organization's commitment to security and can help prevent breaches by ensuring that the entire organization understands the importance of regulatory requirements.

Navigating the global regulatory landscape requires a proactive approach to compliance. By understanding the key regulations like GDPR and CCPA, and learning from real-world examples such as Marriott International, organizations are better prepared to meet cyberattacks.

Sector-Specific Regulations: Addressing Industry-Specific Cybersecurity Needs

In addition to general data protection laws like GDPR and CCPA, certain industries are subject to sector-specific regulations due to the sensitivity and critical nature of the data they handle. These regulations are designed to address the unique vulnerabilities and risks associated with specific types of data, such as healthcare records and financial transactions. This section explores two sector-specific regulations, HIPAA and PCI DSS, which exemplify the stringent standards set for industries handling highly sensitive information.

Health Insurance Portability and Accountability

In the United States, the Health Insurance Portability and Accountability Act, or HIPAA, sets the standard for the protection of sensitive patient data. Enacted in 1996, HIPAA requires healthcare providers, insurers and their business associates to ensure the confidentiality, integrity and availability of protected health information (PHI). Key provisions of HIPAA include:

Privacy Rule: Regulates who may use and share PHI.

Security Rule: Requires appropriate administrative, physical and technical safeguards to ensure the confidentiality, integrity and security of electronic PHI.

Breach Notification Rule: Mandates that those entities and their business associates which fall under the act must notify patients following a breach of unsecured PHI.

Compliance with HIPAA both protects patient privacy and the organization. Non-compliance exposes an organization to potential fines and other legal consequences.

Payment Card Industry Data Security Standard

The Payment Card Industry Data Security Standard (PCI DSS) is a global regulation that aims to secure credit and debit card transactions against data theft and fraud. It applies to all entities that store, process or transmit cardholder data, from large corporations to small vendors. PCI DSS compliance is enforced by the major credit card companies, including Visa, MasterCard, American Express and Discover. PCI DSS requirements include:

Maintaining a Secure Network: Installing and maintaining a firewall configuration to protect cardholder data.

Protecting Cardholder Data: Ensuring that cardholder data is protected when stored and transmitted across open, public networks.

Implementing Strong Access Control Measures: Restricting access to cardholder data by business need-to-know.

Regular Monitoring and Testing: Tracking and monitoring all access to network resources and cardholder data to ensure that all security measures remain effective.

Anthem's HIPPA Compliance Efforts

In 2015, Anthem Inc., one of the largest health insurance providers in the U.S., suffered a massive data breach that exposed the sensitive information of nearly 80 million individuals. The company's failure to secure the information of its customers led to significant financial penalties and prompted the company to do a major overhaul of its cybersecurity practices, specifically around HIPAA compliance. The overhaul started with assessing and improving its data security framework, which led to upgrading its encryption methods, tightening access controls, and implementing more robust data-monitoring systems.[2]

Sector-specific regulations like HIPAA and PCI DSS demonstrate the importance of tailored cybersecurity strategies that address the particular risks associated with different types of sensitive data. For organizations operating within these regulated sectors, compliance is a necessary requirement that safeguards the interests of consumers and protects the organization's reputation and financial well-being.

Compliance Strategies: Navigating the Regulatory Maze

While navigating the complex landscape of cybersecurity regulations can be a daunting task for many organizations, the implementation of effective compliance measures has multiple benefits. In sum, by meeting the required standards, businesses are made more resilient against cyber threats. Here are some reasons why.

Dedicated Compliance Teams

One of the most effective strategies for managing regulatory compliance is the creation of dedicated compliance teams. These teams are tasked with staying up-to-date on all relevant laws and regulations that impact the organization. Their responsibilities include:

Regulatory Monitoring: Keeping track of changes in cybersecurity laws and regulations at state, national and international levels.

Policy Implementation: Translating regulatory requirements into company policies and procedures. This involves working closely with IT, legal and operational departments to ensure that compliance measures are integrated seamlessly into daily business processes.

Training and Awareness: Educating employees about compliance requirements and the importance of following established protocols to protect the organization from potential legal and financial penalties.

Dedicated compliance teams serve as the cornerstone of an effective regulatory strategy, ensuring that all aspects of compliance are continuously addressed and that the organization remains proactive rather than reactive in its compliance efforts.

Regular Audits

Regular internal and external audits are critical to ensuring that compliance measures are put into place and are being adhered to throughout an organization. As well, regular audits help identify compliance gaps and provide opportunities for continuous improvement. An effective audit strategy should include:

Internal Audits: Conducted by the organization's own compliance team, these audits allow for ongoing monitoring and quick rectification of compliance issues.

External Audits: Engaging third-party auditors can provide an unbiased assessment of the organization's compliance status. External auditors bring a fresh perspective and can help benchmark the organization's practices against industry standards and best practices.

Barclays Bank Compliance Strategy

A case study that exemplifies effective compliance strategies is Barclays Bank. Faced with stringent regulatory requirements across multiple countries, Barclays has developed a comprehensive compliance program that includes a dedicated group risk compliance team. This team is responsible for monitoring regulatory changes, advising on compliance matters, and ensuring that all business units adhere to both internal policies and external legal requirements. Furthermore, Barclays regularly conducts both internal and external audits to verify compliance across all departments. These audits are critical in identifying any discrepancies or areas of improvement, allowing Barclays to maintain high standards of compliance consistently.[3]

Compliance strategies, such as having dedicated compliance teams and regular audits, help ensure organizations are following the rules and have the related benefit of strengthening protocols to mitigate cyber threats and support sustainable business growth.

Data Sovereignty and Localization: Adapting to Geographical Compliance Requirements

In the global digital economy, data sovereignty and localization are becoming increasingly critical components of cybersecurity compliance. Certain regulations mandate that data be stored and processed within specific geographical boundaries to protect privacy and maintain national security. For multinational corporations or any organization dealing with data on an international scale, understanding and adhering to these requirements is necessary to avoid legal penalties and to maintain trust with users and regulators. This section explores the strategies for compliance with data sovereignty and localization laws, including data mapping and the use of localized data centers.

Data Mapping

The first step in complying with data sovereignty and localization requirements is to pinpoint where all data resides within the organization. This process, known as data mapping, involves identifying not just where primary data is stored, but also where backups, archives and copies exist, including those stored in the cloud. Data mapping should cover:

Identification of Data Types: Understanding what types of data are collected (e.g., personal, sensitive, corporate) and the applicable regulatory requirements for each.

Geographical Data Flows: Mapping how data moves between systems and borders, which is crucial for ensuring compliance when data crosses international lines.

Audit and Documentation: Regular audits verify the accuracy of the data map and updating documentation to reflect any changes in data storage or processing practices.

Data mapping provides a clear picture of the data landscape, aiding in the strategic planning of data storage and processing to meet localization requirements.

Localized Data Centers

For organizations that handle data subject to localization laws, establishing or partnering with data centers in the required jurisdictions is a practical solution. Localized data centers ensure that Data is processed and stored within the geographical boundaries stipulated by law, thereby simplifying compliance. Key considerations include:

Selecting Reputable Providers: Choosing data center providers that have a strong track record of compliance and security in the required region.

Scalability and Flexibility: Ensuring that the data centers can scale and adapt to the changing needs and growth of the organization.

Security and Reliability: Verifying that the data centers meet high standards of security and operational reliability.

Amazon Web Services and Data Localization

Amazon Web Services has responded to the increasing demand for localized data solutions by establishing data centers in numerous countries around the world, including those with strict data localization laws like Germany, India and Canada. AWS provides customers with the flexibility to choose where their Data is stored and processed, ensuring compliance with national laws and regulations. This global network of data centers ensures that AWS is meeting regulatory requirements and is offering its customers reliable service by reducing latency for local users.[4]

Navigating the complexities of data sovereignty and localization requires careful planning and strategic investment. Through mapping data flows and investing in localized data centers, organizations can better ensure compliance with geographic-specific regulations, safeguarding themselves against legal repercussions and reinforcing their commitment to data privacy and security. This approach not only meets legal obligations but also builds trust with customers by demonstrating a commitment to protecting their data according to the highest standards.

How to Stay Informed of New Compliance Frameworks

Government oversight of compliance means that regulations are continuously evolving to keep pace with the latest threats and technological advancements. Staying informed of these changes is a necessity for organizations aiming to maintain compliance and safeguard their operations. Two important tactics are using regulatory alerts and ongoing education of personnel.

Regulatory Alerts

One of the most efficient methods for staying informed about changes in the regulatory landscape is to subscribe to regulatory alerts. These alerts can come from a variety of sources:

Government Agencies and Regulatory Bodies: Many regulators offer subscription-based services that send updates directly via email or through their websites. These can include broad updates on regulatory changes or specific guidance on compliance requirements.

Industry Associations: Trade associations often provide members with targeted updates that are specific to their sector. These updates can help organizations understand how new regulations might impact their specific industry.

Legal and Compliance Consultancies: These firms specialize in tracking and interpreting regulatory changes. Subscribing to their newsletters or alerts can provide valuable insights into complex regulatory developments and offer practical advice on compliance strategies.

By staying connected to these sources, organizations can receive timely updates that help them adjust their policies and procedures accordingly.

Training and Workshops

Regular training sessions and workshops ensure that key personnel understand any new regulatory changes and how they impact the organization. These educational sessions should cover:

Understanding New Regulations: Detailed explanations of what the new regulations entail, the rationale behind them, and the deadlines for compliance.

Practical Implications: Discussions on how the changes will affect current operational processes and what steps need to be taken to ensure compliance.

Interactive Scenarios: Workshops that include scenario-based training can help staff better understand the application of regulations in real-world contexts.

Training should be an ongoing process, adjusted as new information becomes available and as regulatory requirements evolve.

Salesforce's Compliance Strategy

Being a global leader in customer relationship management software, Salesforce operates in multiple countries, each with its own set of data protection and privacy laws. To manage this complex regulatory ecosystem, Salesforce implemented a robust compliance program that includes a dedicated legal team responsible for monitoring regulatory changes across the globe. The company uses a combination of internal briefings and external legal consultations to stay current.

Salesforce also conducts regular training sessions for its staff, ensuring that each team understands the compliance requirements relevant to their specific roles. These sessions are augmented with online resources and tools that employees can access to refresh their knowledge as needed.

* * *

Maintaining compliance in a dynamic and intricate regulatory environment requires a proactive approach to learning and adaptation. By leveraging regulatory alerts and conducting regular training, organizations can ensure that they remain informed and prepared for any changes. This ongoing commitment to compliance not only helps avoid legal penalties but also reinforces an organization's reputation for reliability and trustworthiness.

With this regulatory framework in mind, we'll transition to an increasingly hot topic—Artificial Intelligence in Cybersecurity. Artificial intelligence is revolutionizing threat detection and response mechanisms, providing tools that are not only faster but also more intelligent in identifying and mitigating cyber threats. However, a big question is whether AI can keep up with the criminal element that can turn AI to its advantage too.

ENDNOTES

1   "Marriott International GDPR Fine: What Did We Learn?" (lawyermonthly.com), https://www.lawyer-monthly.com/2020/11/18-4-million-marriott-international-gdpr-fine-announced-by-ipo-what-did-we-learn/ ICO statement: Intention to fine Marriott International, Inc. more than £99 million under GDPR for data breach | European Data Protection Board (europa.eu), https://www.edpb.europa.eu/news/nationalnews/2019/ico-statement-intention-fine-marriott-international-inc-more-ps99-million_en.

2   "Anthem Pays OCR $16 Million in Record HIPAA Settlement," HHS.gov, https://www.hhs.gov/for-professionals/compliance-enforcement/agreeements/anthm/index.html.

3   "Latest News on Barclays: Regulatory Challenges, Strategic Partnerships, and Technological Advancements," Fintech Energy, https://fintech.energy/latest-news-on-barclays-regulatory-challenges-strategicpartnerships-and-technological-advancements/.

4   "Does data localization cause more problems than it solves?", Whitepaper, AWS Security Blog (amazon.com), https://aws.amazon.com/blogs/security/introducing-a-new-aws-whitepaperdoes-data-localization-cause-more-problems-than-it-solves/.

CHAPTER 12

ARTIFICIAL INTELLIGENCE IN CYBERSECURITY

Artificial intelligence (AI) has rapidly emerged as a transformative force across industries, including how we understand and engage with cybersecurity. This chapter explores the multifaceted role of AI in enhancing cybersecurity measures, focusing on its capabilities to analyze vast amounts of data, make predictive analyses and automate complex tasks. Detailed examinations of AI applications in threat detection, response automation and ethical considerations are discussed along with an example of a leading financial institution that used AI in a real-world cybersecurity operation.

AI-Powered Threat Detection

Artificial intelligence has revolutionized the field of threat detection within cybersecurity by employing advanced algorithms that are capable of identifying patterns and anomalies that often escape traditional detection methods.[1] In this section, we will discuss behavioral analytics, predictive analysis and the integration of AI across cybersecurity frameworks.

Behavioral Analytics

One of the core strengths of AI in cybersecurity is its ability to conduct behavioral analytics. This process involves monitoring and analyzing user behaviors to detect deviations from normal activity patterns. AI systems are equipped with the capability to learn what constitutes normal behavior for each user over time, creating a personalized behavioral baseline.

These AI systems continuously monitor user activities, including login times, the frequency and type of accessed files, and typical network actions.

When AI detects activity that deviates from established norms, it flags these events as potential security threats. For instance, if a user typically accesses certain databases during regular business hours, but suddenly attempts to download large volumes of sensitive data at midnight, the AI system would flag this activity as suspicious. This capability enables organizations to respond proactively to potential threats, often before any real damage can be done.

Predictive Analysis

Predictive analysis works by aggregating and analyzing historical security data, including past breaches, common security incidents and previously detected threats. By applying machine learning models, AI can identify patterns and trends that are indicative of future threats. For example, if an analysis of historical data shows that certain types of phishing attacks spike during specific times of the year, the AI system can alert administrators to heighten their security measures during these periods.

Furthermore, AI-driven predictive analysis can extend to predicting the behavior of potential cyber threats once they enter the network. By understanding how similar threats have progressed in the past, AI can forecast the likely paths an attack will take, enabling faster containment and more precise targeting of defensive measures.

Implementation and Integration

Implementing AI in threat detection involves integrating these systems with existing cybersecurity infrastructure. This integration allows AI tools to access the necessary data streams from network traffic, user activity logs and security event management systems for effective monitoring and analysis.

For AI-powered threat detection to function optimally, it must be backed by high-quality comprehensive data. This requires organizations to invest in AI technology and in the infrastructure and processes that support effective data collection and management. The effectiveness of AI-driven threat detection heavily relies on the quality of data used for training its algorithms.

Phishing Detection

Phishing attacks remain one of the most pervasive and insidious forms of cyber threats that organizations encounter today due to their relatively low cost and the ease with which they can be deployed. Artificial intelligence has become a potent ally in the fight against these threats, offering capabilities that go far beyond the reach of traditional methods.

Email Analysis with AI

AI has transformed email security by enabling deeper and more nuanced analysis of incoming messages. Traditional spam filters, which primarily rely on simple rules and signature matching, often fall short when it comes to detecting sophisticated phishing attempts. In contrast, AI-driven systems assess emails on multiple levels, including their context, structure and the behavior patterns of the sender.

> **Contextual Analysis**: AI examines the context of each email by understanding the typical content and style of communications within an organization. It looks for anomalies in language use, subtle cues in tone, or unusual requests that could indicate a phishing attempt.

> **Structural Analysis**: AI algorithms analyze the structure of an email, including its header information, embedded links and attachments. It scrutinizes how these elements are constructed—such as the authenticity of the domain names in links or the presence of file types commonly associated with malware.

> **Sender Behavior Analysis**: By creating profiles based on normal email activity, AI can detect deviations that may suggest impersonation or malicious intent. For example, an email that claims to be from a senior executive but originates from an unusual IP address or has been sent at an unusual hour might be flagged for further scrutiny.

These AI capabilities ensure a comprehensive assessment of potential threats, significantly reducing the likelihood of phishing emails reaching their intended targets.

Website Analysis with AI

AI's role extends beyond email to include real-time scanning of websites for phishing indicators. This is important because phishing websites often mimic legitimate sites to trick users into entering sensitive information.

Real-Time Scanning: AI systems continuously scan websites accessed by users, looking for signs of phishing. These signs can include suspicious domain registrations, security certificate anomalies, or webpage layouts that replicate well-known sites but which contain malicious content.

Behavioral Analysis of Websites: AI analyzes the behavior of web pages, checking for scripts or redirects that are typical of phishing sites. This analysis helps identify malicious sites even before any user data is compromised.

Dynamic Learning: As AI systems encounter new types of phishing tactics, they learn and adapt. This dynamic learning process continuously improves the AI's ability to detect and respond to emerging threats.

Integration with Cybersecurity Frameworks

Integrating AI-driven phishing detection tools into broader cybersecurity frameworks amplifies their effectiveness. These tools work alongside other defensive measures, providing a layered security approach that significantly hardens an organization's defenses against cyber threats.

Data Sharing: AI systems can share insights and data about new threats with other components of the cybersecurity framework, such as firewalls and intrusion detection systems, creating a cohesive and informed response mechanism across all levels of IT security.

User Training and Awareness: AI tools can also support cybersecurity training programs by providing real-world examples of phishing attempts and guiding users on how to respond. This helps foster a culture of security awareness throughout the organization.[2]

Ethical Considerations in AI-Enabled Cybersecurity

The integration of AI into cybersecurity brings with it not only technological advancements but also ethical challenges. These challenges primarily revolve around data privacy and the transparency and accountability of AI systems. As these systems become more integral to security infrastructures, ethical issues must be surfaced to maintain public trust and compliance with legal standards.

Data Privacy

AI systems are inherently data-driven, relying on vast amounts of information to train algorithms and make decisions. This dependency poses significant privacy concerns, particularly regarding the collection, storage and usage of sensitive data:

Consent and Collection: Ensuring that data used by AI systems is collected with informed consent is fundamental. Users must be aware of what data is being collected and for what purpose. This transparency is not just an ethical requirement but often a legal one, as seen in regulations like the GDPR in Europe and CCPA in California.

Data Minimization and Retention: Ethical AI practices dictate that only the necessary data for a defined purpose should be collected, and data should be retained only as long as needed. This principle of data minimization helps protect user privacy and reduces the risk of data breaches.

Secure Storage and Access: Protecting stored data with the latest security measures is crucial. AI systems must implement robust encryption and access controls to prevent unauthorized data access and ensure the integrity and confidentiality of user information.

Transparency and Accountability

AI systems in cybersecurity must operate transparently to generate user trust and be held accountable for their actions for regulatory compliance. There must be:

Oversight of AI Decisions: There should be clarity on how AI systems make decisions, especially when these decisions impact user security or privacy. Oversight is necessary for auditing and regulatory purposes and helps in identifying any biases or errors in the AI algorithms.

Accountability Mechanisms: There must be mechanisms in place to hold AI systems and their operators accountable for the decisions made. This involves clear documentation of decision-making processes and criteria, regular audits of AI systems, and protocols for addressing any issues or failures.

Addressing AI Bias: AI systems are only as unbiased as the data they are trained on. Ensuring that AI algorithms are trained on diverse, representative datasets is necessary to minimize bias. Regular testing and updating of these systems can help address biases that may arise as the AI learns and evolves.

Creating an Ethical AI Framework

Creating an ethical AI framework involves several stakeholders, including ethicists, technologists, legal experts and end-users. This framework should guide the development and deployment of AI systems in cybersecurity, ensuring they respect user privacy, operate transparently and remain accountable for their actions.[3]

Stakeholder Engagement: Regular engagement with stakeholders can help identify potential ethical issues early on and ensure that the AI systems align with broader societal values and legal standards.

Continuous Monitoring and Evaluation: As AI technologies evolve, so too should the strategies for their ethical use. Continuous monitoring and evaluation of AI systems help ensure that they adapt to new ethical challenges and technological advancements.

AI in Action Against Cyber Threats

The rapid evolution of cyber threats necessitates equally advanced defense mechanisms. As we learn from the example of a leading financial institution below, it leveraged AI to thwart a complex attack aimed at its transaction processing system, highlighting the effectiveness of AI in modern cybersecurity.[4]

This financial institution, known for its advanced security measures, faced an unprecedented challenge when cybercriminals targeted its transaction processing system. The attackers employed sophisticated techniques to mimic legitimate user activities, aiming to bypass traditional security protocols unnoticed.

The institution's conventional security systems were structured around known threat signatures and typical anomaly detection, which proved insufficient against the advanced tactics used by the attackers. These methods failed to detect the subtle, yet abnormal, behaviors embedded within legitimate processes, posing a significant threat to the integrity of the institution's financial operations.

Recognizing the limitations of its existing security measures, the institution turned to AI for a solution. It deployed an AI system equipped to analyze complex transaction patterns and detect anomalies that deviate from established norms. The specific AI technology implemented included machine learning algorithms capable of continuous learning and adaptation, enhancing its ability to respond to new threats as they evolve.

AI was trained on extensive datasets encompassing years of transaction histories and user behaviors, enabling it to learn and recognize the intricacies of normal operations versus potential threats. The AI system was integrated with the institution's existing cybersecurity infrastructure, ensuring that it could interact with real-time transaction data and other relevant security systems for comprehensive monitoring.

The AI system proved to be exceptionally effective. It successfully identified unusual transaction patterns that subtly deviated from the norm—patterns that had initially gone unnoticed by traditional systems. Upon detection of these anomalies, the AI system automatically initiated a detailed audit of the affected transactions and temporarily froze suspicious activities to prevent further unauthorized access. Security teams immediately began to conduct a thorough investigation, revealing a coordinated attack designed to siphon funds through carefully disguised transactions.

Thanks to the rapid response enabled by AI, the institution prevented significant financial losses and averted damage to its reputation. The incident prompted a comprehensive review of existing security protocols and the adoption of more AI-driven security measures across other critical systems.

This example underscores several critical lessons:

Proactive Detection: AI's capability to analyze and interpret vast amounts of data in real-time is indispensable in identifying threats that mimic legitimate activities.

Integration of AI: Effective cybersecurity is no longer just about having the right tools but integrating them in a manner that allows for seamless communication and real-time response capabilities.

Continuous Improvement: Continuous training of AI systems with updated data and threat scenarios contributes to maintaining the efficacy of these systems. AI has demonstrated its capability as a cornerstone of modern cybersecurity strategies.

By incorporating AI, organizations can enhance their ability to detect, analyze and respond to increasingly sophisticated cyber threats, thereby securing their digital and financial assets more effectively. This serves as a compelling example of AI's transformative impact on cybersecurity, offering valuable insights for institutions worldwide seeking to bolster their defenses against advanced cyber threats. Artificial intelligence has been tested and has emerged as a technology capable of detecting and responding to sophisticated cyber-attacks.

The Privacy Concern

As artificial intelligence continues to evolve, its integration into the cybersecurity domain becomes increasingly significant. This transformative technology offers significant advantages for enhancing threat detection capabilities, automating responses and improving ethical governance practices. However, the deployment of AI in cybersecurity also involves navigating complex challenges and potential ethical implications. For organizations aiming to harness AI's full potential, a balanced and carefully considered approach is essential.

AI's capabilities in analyzing vast data sets allow it to identify subtle patterns and anomalies that might elude human analysts and conventional software systems. This capacity for enhanced detection is particularly valuable given the sophisticated nature of modern cyber threats, which often involve tactics designed to mimic legitimate activities or hide within large volumes of legitimate data traffic. Moreover, AI can provide predictive insights, not just reactive analyses, enabling organizations to anticipate and mitigate potential threats before they materialize. This proactive stance in cybersecurity can drastically reduce the incidence and impact of breaches.

However, the power of AI to autonomously analyze and act upon data also raises significant ethical and operational challenges. One of the foremost concerns is the issue of privacy. AI systems typically require access to extensive data to function optimally, which can include sensitive personal information. Ensuring that Data is handled in compliance with both local and international data protection regulations (such as GDPR or CCPA) is crucial. Moreover, there is a risk that AI could inadvertently breach privacy guidelines due to its capacity to infer new information from available data sets.

The Bias Concern

Another challenge lies in the potential for AI systems to be biased. AI models can only be as unbiased as the data on which they are trained. If any source data contain inherent biases—perhaps due to skewed sample populations or prejudiced historical decisions—these biases will be perpetuated and amplified by AI systems. Such issues can lead to discriminatory practices or unjust outcomes, which can be difficult to detect and rectify given the opaque nature of some AI decision-making processes.

To address these challenges, transparency and accountability must be at the forefront of any AI deployment in cybersecurity. Organizations need to ensure that they can audit AI systems and explain their decisions when necessary, particularly in situations where a decision leads to significant consequences. This transparency is essential for maintaining public trust and complying with legal standards that might require explanations of automated decisions.

Furthermore, the ability of AI to automate responses to detected threats can also pose risks. Automated actions taken without human oversight might result in unintended consequences, such as the wrongful blocking of legitimate user activities or data access. Implementing safeguards, such as thresholds for when human intervention is required, can help mitigate these risks.

* * *

As AI becomes a more integrated part of the cybersecurity landscape, organizations must adopt a proactive and informed approach to its deployment. They can do this by leveraging AI's capabilities to enhance security measures and concurrently addressing the ethical and practical challenges associated with its use. This balanced approach will bolster cybersecurity defenses and support sustainable, long-term security strategies that protect against both current and emerging threats.

Next, our focus shifts from the broader capabilities of AI to the specific challenges and strategies related to securing cloud environments. This chapter will delve into the nuances of cloud security, examining how the principles of cybersecurity must be adapted to protect data and operations in cloud-based systems, which are becoming central to organizational IT strategies across the globe.

Endnotes

1 "AI in Cybersecurity: Revolutionizing Threat Detection," https://datasciencedojo.com/blog/ai-incybersecurity/.

2 Lesline Gilzene, "Implementing Cybersecurity Frameworks: Strengthening Defenses and Mitigating Risks," CyberForum, https://medium.com/cyberforum/implementing-cybersecurity-frameworks-strengthening-defenses-and-mitigating-risks-d667be627b20.

3 "What is AI Ethics?", IBM, https://www.ibm.com/topics/aiethics.

4 "How Artificial Intelligence (AI) Can Help With Cybersecurity Threats: Fortinet Defends Against Cyber Threats with AI Solutions from Microsoft," Microsoft Industry Blogs, https://www.microsoft.com/ enus/industry/blog/government/defense-and-intelligence/2024/03/07/defend-against-cyber-threats-with-ai-solutions-from-microsoft/.

Chapter 13

The Growing Importance of Cloud Security

The migration to cloud computing has revolutionized the way organizations operate, offering scalability, flexibility and significant cost savings. However, as data and operations increasingly shift to the cloud, organizations must increase their vigilance to protect their assets. We'll focus on the aspects of cloud security in this chapter, which are both relational and technological.

Understanding the Shared Responsibility Model

In the realm of cloud computing, the concept of security is fundamentally underpinned by the shared responsibility model—a framework that delineates the roles and responsibilities of the cloud service provider (CSP) and the client. A main goal is to find potential gaps in security protocols that could potentially be exploited by cyber criminals.

The Provider's Responsibilities

The responsibilities of CSPs are primarily the protection and maintenance of the cloud infrastructure. This infrastructure includes the physical data centers, the servers, the networking hardware and the software systems that enable cloud services. CSPs must ensure that these physical and virtual resources are capable of defending assets against various threats, including cyberattacks, natural disasters and system failures. These resources include:

Physical Security: CSPs are tasked with securing the physical premises of their data centers. This includes deploying security measures such as surveillance cameras, biometric access controls and security personnel to guard against unauthorized physical access.

Server and Hardware Security: Ensuring the security of the hardware that runs cloud services involves maintaining hardware integrity from tampering or damage and implementing secure hardware disposal practices.

Storage Security: Safeguarding data storage involves physical security measures and the implementation of data segmentation and encryption to protect data at rest.

Networking Security: CSPs must secure the networks over which data travel. This includes deploying firewalls, intrusion detection systems and encryption protocols to safeguard data in transit and prevent unauthorized access.

The Client's Responsibilities

While providers manage the security of the cloud infrastructure, clients are responsible for securing everything they put in the cloud. These areas of responsibility include:

Data Security: Clients must protect their data through encryption, both in transit and at rest, to prevent unauthorized access. Additionally, implementing data classification and data loss prevention (DLP) strategies can further enhance the security of sensitive information.

Application Security: Clients are responsible for ensuring that the applications they deploy in the cloud are secure. Security protocols include regular updates and patches to applications to mitigate vulnerabilities.

Access Control: Managing who has access to cloud resources involves implementing identity and access management (IAM) systems that support strong authentication methods, such as multi-factor authentication (MFA), and ensuring that permissions are appropriately assigned based on the principle of least privilege.

Configuration Management: Clients must configure their cloud environments securely by setting security groups and network access controls that align with their organizational security policies.

The shared responsibility model emphasizes that while CSPs provide the tools and services to secure the cloud infrastructure, clients must actively use these tools and follow best practices to secure their applications and data. It's a collaborative partnership in which both parties must engage proactively to maintain a secure cloud environment, which in turn optimizes business outcomes.

Data Protection in the Cloud

In the cloud environment, the integrity and privacy of data must be protected against a variety of cyber threats and technical failures. Effective data protection strategies in the cloud consist of several key components, including encryption, backup and redundancy, access controls and ongoing monitoring. Each of these plays a critical role in safeguarding data from unauthorized access and loss, ensuring that cloud environments remain secure and resilient.[1]

Encryption

Encryption is the cornerstone of data protection in the cloud. It serves as the first line of defense by encoding data in such a way that only authorized parties can access it. Encryption should be applied in two main states:

Data at Rest: Encrypting data at rest ensures that stored data is protected against unauthorized access and theft. This is particularly important in cloud storage, where data is housed in shared environments that could potentially be accessed by malicious actors. Techniques such as advanced encryption standards (AES) are commonly used for encrypting stored data, providing a high level of security.

Data in Transit: As data moves between the user's device and the cloud servers, or between different servers within the cloud, it is susceptible to interception. Encrypting data in transit protects it from being intercepted by unauthorized entities. This is typically achieved using protocols such as Transport Layer Security (TLS) or its predecessor, Secure 221 Socket Layer (SSL), which establish a secure channel over an insecure network.

Backup and Redundancy

To mitigate the risks of data loss due to technical failures, natural disasters or cyber incidents, regular backups and strategic redundancy are essential:

Regular Backups: Implementing a routine backup schedule ensures that copies of Data is available for recovery in the event of data corruption, accidental deletion or a ransomware attack. Cloud providers often offer automated backup services that can be configured to meet specific recovery time objectives (RTOs) and recovery point objectives (RPOs).

Redundancy: Redundancy involves storing multiple copies of data in geographically dispersed locations. This practice, often referred to as geo-redundancy, enhances data availability and durability, meaning that an outage or failure at one site does not result in permanent data loss. Many cloud services use redundant storage to automatically create and manage multiple copies of data, making it an integral aspect of cloud storage solutions.

Access Controls

Ensuring that only authorized users have access to sensitive data is another vital component of cloud data protection. This involves:

Identity and Access Management: IAM systems help manage user identities and govern user access to resources. These systems should possess strong authentication methods and integrate seamlessly with corporate directories to manage identities across the organization.

Role-Based Access Control: RBAC allows organizations to grant access rights based on the roles of individual users within the organization. This approach ensures that users receive access permissions strictly necessary for their job functions, minimizing the risk of unauthorized data exposure.

Monitoring and Alerting

Continuous monitoring and alerting mechanisms are essential for detecting potential security breaches and unauthorized data access attempts in real time. Monitoring systems can identify unusual access patterns or modifications to data, triggering alerts that enable rapid response to potential threats. Security Information and Event Management systems (SEIMs) collect and analyze logs and events from various sources within the cloud environment, providing insights into security incidents and helping with regulatory compliance.

Protecting data in the cloud requires a multifaceted approach that integrates strong encryption, comprehensive backup and redundancy plans, stringent access controls and proactive monitoring.

Access Control in the Cloud

Maintaining stringent access control safeguards cloud resources by ensuring that only authorized users can access sensitive data and systems. As organizations increasingly rely on cloud services, the complexity and importance of effective access control mechanisms, such as Identity and Access Management and Multi-Factor Authentication, continue to grow. These technologies manage who can access what within the cloud, thereby minimizing the risk of data breaches and unauthorized access.[2]

Identity and Access Management

IAM is a framework of business processes, policies and technologies that facilitates the management of electronic identities. In the cloud, IAM systems play a critical role in ensuring that the right individuals access the appropriate resources under the right conditions. These systems are comprehensive, encompassing not just user credentials but also the policies that govern what users are allowed to do with their access. IAM has several components:

User Authentication: IAM systems verify the identity of a user attempting to access the cloud environment. This is typically done through usernames and passwords, although more secure systems also incorporate other forms of verification.

Authorization: Once authenticated, a user must be authorized to access specific resources. This is governed by policies that specify what users can and cannot do within the cloud environment, based on their roles or attributes.

Management of User Rights: As users join, leave or move within an organization, their access rights need to be dynamically managed to reflect their current roles. IAM systems allow administrators to easily assign and revoke access privileges, ensuring users have appropriate access through the lifecycle of their relationship with the organization.

Audit and Compliance Reporting: IAM systems log and monitor all user activities within the cloud environment, facilitating compliance with regulatory requirements and providing valuable data for auditing and forensic analysis.

Multi-Factor Authentication

MFA requires users to provide two or more verification factors to gain access to a cloud resource, enhancing security by combining multiple forms of identification, such as something only the user knows (e.g., a password or PIN); something the user has (e.g., a security token, a smartphone app, or a smart card); or the user's person (e.g., biometric factors, such as fingerprints, facial recognition or iris scans).

By requiring multiple forms of verification, MFA significantly reduces the risk of unauthorized access. Even if one factor (like a password) is compromised, unauthorized users are unlikely to have access to the additional factors, thus safeguarding sensitive data and systems.

Role-Based Access Control

RBAC is another important aspect of access control in the cloud. It restricts system access based on the roles of individual users within an organization. In RBAC:

1. Roles are assigned: Based on job competency, authority and responsibility within the organization.

2. Permissions are attached to roles: Each role has specific permissions that determine the access level to the cloud resources.

3. Users are assigned roles: Users receive access to resources strictly based on their assigned role, making management straightforward and scalable.

Monitoring and Incident Response in the Cloud

Continuous monitoring and a proactive incident response strategy contribute to real-time cyber defense measures. Early detection of cyber threats, when combined with well-defined incident-response protocols, is the backbone of reducing damage cyber incidents can cause.

Cloud Security Monitoring Tools

Cloud security monitoring tools are designed to detect anomalies, unauthorized access attempts and potential security threats as they occur. Their primary features and functions include:

Real-Time Monitoring: These systems continuously scan and analyze cloud environments to identify activities that deviate from the norm, which could indicate potential security issues or breaches.

Threat Detection: Advanced monitoring tools use various methods such as signature-based detection, anomaly detection and behavior analytics to identify malicious activities and potential threats quickly.

Automated Alerts: Upon detecting suspicious activities, these tools generate automatic alerts that notify security personnel. This immediate notification allows for swift action to mitigate threats before they can escalate.

Integration Capabilities: Effective monitoring solutions integrate seamlessly with other security tools and systems, providing a comprehensive view of security posture, and enabling a unified response strategy across various platforms and services.

Incident-Response Protocols

While monitoring tools are designed to detect threats, having a dynamic incident-response protocol is essential for responding effectively to security incidents. These protocols consist of a series of steps to be followed in the event of a security breach or attack, ensuring that actions are swift and coordinated. These steps are as follows:

1. Preparation: Organizations must be prepared for potential security incidents by having all necessary tools, roles and communications plans in place. This preparation includes regular training for all relevant personnel on their roles during an incident.

2. Identification: Being able to quickly determine the nature and scope of an incident means organizations can potentially mitigate the damage from a cyberattack. Identification involves analyzing the security alerts generated by monitoring tools to identify the source, method and impact of the breach.

3. Containment: Once an incident is identified, the immediate priority is to contain it. This may involve isolating affected systems, shutting down certain processes, or revoking access to compromised accounts to prevent further damage.

4. Eradication: After containment, the cause of the incident must be removed from the environment. This could mean deleting

malicious files, disabling breached user accounts, or updating software to eliminate vulnerabilities.

5. Recovery: The focus then shifts to safely restoring and validating system functionality for business operations. This step ensures that all systems are clean and fully operational before they are brought back online.

6. Lessons Learned: After managing an incident, conducting a thorough review is crucial. This review assesses how the incident was handled, what could be improved, and how to better prepare for future incidents. Insights gained are used to strengthen existing protocols and security measures.

Vendor Assessment in Cloud Security

Vendor assessment in cloud security ensures that the selected CSP can adequately protect sensitive data and comply with relevant regulatory standards. The process involves several key components, from initial screening to in-depth evaluations of technical and operational capabilities. This thorough evaluation not only mitigates risks associated with data breaches and cyber threats but also aligns the CSP's capabilities with the organization's strategic goals. Proper due diligence ensures that an organization can select the CSP best positioned to meet the organization's security needs and compliance requirements. This process includes scrutinizing security certifications, reviewing service level agreements (SLAs), and evaluating the CSP's overall security architecture and practices.[3]

Security Certifications

Security certifications signal a CSP's commitment to security. They provide a baseline of trust and ensure that the provider meets specific international standards in their operations and security practices. Here are some of the critical certifications to consider during vendor assessment:

ISO 27001: This is one of the most widely recognized certifications for information security management systems (ISMS). It specifies the requirements for establishing, implementing, maintaining and continually improving an ISMS. A CSP with ISO 27001 certification demonstrates a commitment to managing sensitive company and customer information securely.

SOC 2: This audit specification, developed by the American Institute of CPAs (AICPA), was designed for service providers storing customer data in the cloud. It requires providers to follow strict information security policies and procedures, encompassing the security, availability, processing integrity, confidentiality and privacy of customer data.

PCI DSS: If the organization processes, stores or transmits credit card information, PCI DSS compliance cannot be understated. This standard helps in securing and protecting payment card data.

General Data Protection Regulation Compliance: Organizations operating in or dealing with data from the European Union must comply with GDPR. This regulation mandates strict data protection and privacy for individuals within the EU and the European Economic Area.

These certifications should be viewed as minimum requirements, not the sole criteria for selection, as they provide a starting point for understanding the CSP's approach to security and data protection.

Service-Level Agreements

Service-level agreements are another critical aspect of the vendor assessment process. SLAs outline the specific commitments made by the CSP regarding the performance and reliability of their services. Main aspects of SLAs include:

Uptime Commitments: SLAs should specify the guaranteed uptime, which is crucial for business continuity. Higher uptime guarantees (typically expressed as percentages like 99.99%) indicate more reliable service.

Data Protection: It's essential to understand how the CSP will protect data. This includes their data backup processes, data redundancy practices, and disaster recovery procedures.

Security Incident Responses: The SLA should clearly outline how the CSP will respond to security incidents, including the expected response times and the types of support available during a security breach.

Penalty Clauses: Consider the penalties or compensations offered if the provider fails to meet their SLA commitments. This can serve as an incentive for the provider to uphold high standards.

Evaluating Security Practices and Architecture

Beyond certifications and SLAs, it's necessary to assess the CSP's security architecture and practices, such as:

Physical Security: Review the physical security measures in place at the CSP's data centers.

Data Encryption Practices: Ensure that the CSP employs robust encryption methods for data at rest and in transit.

Regular Security Audits: Check if the CSP conducts regular security audits and vulnerability assessments.

Employee Security Training: Assess the provider's commitment to security training for their employees.

Securing the Cloud Infrastructure of a Financial Services firm

A leading financial services firm, operating globally, faced significant challenges in securing its expansive cloud-based data repositories. These repositories housed sensitive client information and were distributed across multiple regions, increasing the complexity of the security measures required. The firm's cloud infrastructure needed to not only protect sensitive financial data but also comply with stringent regulatory requirements across different jurisdictions, including GDPR in Europe and SEC regulations in the United States.[4]

The primary challenge was ensuring the security of the cloud environments amidst increasing cyber threats such as data breaches, ransomware attacks and phishing schemes. The financial services sector is particularly attractive to cybercriminals due to the sensitive nature of the data involved. Additionally, the firm had to navigate a complex regulatory landscape that demanded compliance with multiple international data protection and privacy laws.

To address these challenges, the firm embarked on a comprehensive strategy to bolster its cloud security framework, focusing on six measures:

1. Robust Identity and Access Management Implementation: The firm implemented a state-of-the-art IAM system designed to manage user access with precision. This system was configured to enforce role-based access control (RBAC), ensuring that employees could only access data necessary for their specific roles. The IAM solution was integrated with the firm's existing HR systems to automate the management of access rights throughout the employee lifecycle, from onboarding through to off-boarding.

2. Deployment of Multi-Factor Authentication: To further secure access to its cloud environments, the firm deployed MFA across all levels of the organization. MFA was required not only for internal employees but also for external contractors and business partners, ensuring that multiple layers of authentication protected all access points into the cloud environment.

3. Enhanced Encryption Practices: The firm adopted advanced encryption protocols to protect data both at rest and in transit. This included the use of AES-256 encryption for data at rest and TLS 1.3 for data in transit. These encryption standards ensured that even if data was intercepted, it would remain secure and unreadable without the appropriate decryption keys.

4. Real-Time Threat Detection: Investing in advanced monitoring tools, the firm implemented a real-time threat detection system that used machine learning algorithms to identify and respond to potential security threats automatically. This system was integrated with a Security Information and Event Management (SIEM) platform to provide a comprehensive view of all security logs and alerts.

5. Regular Compliance Audits: To ensure ongoing compliance with both internal security policies and external regulatory requirements, the firm established a routine of regular compliance audits. These audits were conducted by both internal audit teams and external third parties. The audits helped identify any gaps in compliance and recommended corrective actions to maintain rigorous security standards.

6. Continuous Security Training: Recognizing the importance of human factors in cybersecurity, the firm also implemented an ongoing security training program. This program was designed to educate employees about security best practices, phishing prevention, and the importance of data protection. Regular training sessions and security drills were scheduled to keep security awareness high.

The implementation of these security measures positioned the firm to be more resilient in the event of a cyberattack. The measures also ensured the organization met its compliance obligations and demonstrated a commitment to protecting client data, thereby reinforcing its reputation in the financial sector.

* * *

While cloud computing offers numerous benefits, it also presents complex security challenges, particularly in sensitive sectors like financial services. By understanding these challenges and implementing comprehensive, tailored security measures, organizations can effectively harness the advantages of cloud computing while ensuring that their data and operations remain secure.

The example of the financial services firm illustrates the successful application of these strategies and demonstrates the importance of having and implementing a strategy. This approach not only safeguards data but also aligns with business objectives, ensuring that security is a business enabler rather than a hurdle.

We now move from the virtual to the tangible. Physical security measures are essential in complementing digital defense measures. Despite the shift towards digital assets, the physical security of hardware, data centers and other critical infrastructure remains a cornerstone of comprehensive security strategies, ensuring that the digital fortifications are effectively supported by real-world protections.

Endnotes

1 "What Is Cloud Data Protection? Benefits & Best Practices," https://www.digitalguardian. com/blog/what-cloud-data-protection-benefits-best-practices.

2 What Is Access Control in Cloud Computing?", BAASS, https://www.baass.com/faq/what-is-access-control-in-cloud-computing Access control, Cloud Adoption Framework, Microsoft Learn, https://learn.microsoft.com/en-us/azure/cloud-adoptionframework/secure/access-control.

3 "The Vendor Security Assessment (VSA): What You Need to Know," Tripwire, "Four Important Best Practices for Assessing Cloud Vendors," cloudsecurityalliance.org, https://www.tripwire.com/state-ofsecurity/the-vendor-security-assessment-vsa-need-to-know; "Four Important Best Practices for Assessing Cloud Vendors," cloudsecurityalliance.org, https://cloudsecurityalliance.org/blog/2017/11/24/ four-important-best-practices-assessing-cloud-vendors; "Vendor Security Risk Assessment," Google Cloud, https://cloud.google.com/security/vendor-security-assessment.

4 "Cloud Security for Financial Services: Protecting Sensitive Data," Unicloud, https://unicloud.co/ blog/cloud-security-for-financialservices-protecting-sensitive-data; "4 Cloud Security Considerations for Financial Services Firms," The New Stack, https://thenewstack.io/4-cloud-security-considerations-forfinancial-services-firms/.

Chapter 14

The Role of Physical Security in a Digital World

In the last chapter we discussed security in the cloud and the vulnerabilities that exist across a supply chain. Cloud security is one part of the equation; the other part is physical security. While invisible cyber threats are ever-evolving, the need to safeguard the tangible assets that house and manage our digital worlds is equally vital. What steps can organizations take to reduce cyber threat risk in the physical ecosystem? This chapter examines best practices of organizations which serve as instructive guidelines for all.

Data Center Security

Data centers store vast amounts of data and are essential for the uninterrupted operation of essential operations. Due to their importance as critical infrastructure, these facilities must be safeguarded with comprehensive security measures to protect against a variety of threats, ranging from physical intrusion to environmental hazards. Implementing resilient physical security measures goes a long way to protecting the integrity and availability of the data housed within these centers.[1]

Access Control Systems

Unassailable access control is elemental to data center security. These systems are designed to ensure that only authorized personnel can enter a premises, and rely on both technology and human interaction.

> **Biometric Systems**: Advanced biometric systems such as fingerprint and retina scanners offer a high level of security by ensuring that only individuals whose biometric data is registered in the system can access sensitive areas. These systems are difficult to spoof, making them one of the most secure forms of access control.

Card Readers: Traditional card readers still play a vital role in access control. Cards can be programmed to provide personnel with varying levels of access to the data center.

Security Personnel: Security personnel can monitor access points and conduct physical checks to ensure that everyone entering the data center has proper authorization. They also play a significant role in emergency response and enforcing security protocols.

Surveillance Systems

Surveillance is another pillar of data center security, providing real-time monitoring of the physical environment. Aspects of surveillance include:

CCTV Monitoring: Continuous video surveillance via CCTV systems equipped with motion detection technology allows for the monitoring of all activities around the data center. CCTV systems can alert security personnel to unusual activities, helping to quickly identify and respond to potential security breaches.

Integrated Alarm Systems: Alarm systems integrated with CCTV surveillance can trigger alerts in response to unauthorized access attempts, enabling rapid deployment of security measures.

Record Keeping: Surveillance footage is also invaluable for post-incident investigations, helping to identify perpetrators and understand the sequence of events during a security breach.

Environmental Controls

Environmental controls are designed to maintain optimal conditions within the data center and prevent damage from fire, water or excessive temperatures. Protecting data centers from environmental threats is as important as defending them from human intrusions.

Fire Suppression Systems: Fire suppression systems are designed to extinguish fires quickly without damaging the sensitive electronic equipment within the facility. They often use chemical agents or inert gases instead of water to prevent damage to hardware.

Climate Control: Data centers generate a lot of heat. HVAC systems ensure that the data center remains at optimal temperatures and humidity levels, thus safeguarding equipment from heat damage and reducing the likelihood of hardware failure.

Flood Prevention: In areas prone to flooding, data centers must incorporate flood prevention measures. This can include elevated buildings, waterproof barriers and drainage systems designed to divert water away from critical infrastructure.

Redundancy and Backup Systems

Redundancy is a key aspect of data center security and operational integrity. Two examples of redundancy within a data center ecosystem are power redundancy and data backups.

Data centers should have redundant power supplies, such as uninterruptible power supplies (UPS) and backup generators, to ensure continuous operation during power outages. Regular data backups are essential for recovery after data loss incidents. These backups should be stored in multiple locations, including offsite storage, to protect against data loss from local disasters.[2]

Regular Audits and Compliance

Regular security audits are vital to maintaining the security integrity of data centers. These audits help identify vulnerabilities and ensure compliance with industry standards and regulations, and may include security audits, which are routine inspections and audits of physical security measures, and which can reveal potential weaknesses and guide improvements.

Additionally, data centers often need to comply with various industry standards, such as ISO/IEC 27001 or the Data Center Standard by the Uptime Institute. Compliance ensures that the data centers meet international security and operational standards.

Securing a data center encompasses a wide range of measures, from advanced access controls and surveillance to environmental protections and regulatory compliance. Together, these measures form a comprehensive security strategy that protects digital assets from physical and environmental threats. As technology and threats evolve, so must the approaches to data center security, ensuring they remain resilient against all forms of risks.

Device Security

Much of today's workforce works outside of a traditional office environment. Those who like to travel can work from destinations that offer perks such as a healthy climate and surf and sand. All one needs is a mobile device, laptop and connectivity. This shift brings with it significant convenience and flexibility, but also introduces a range of security risks. Devices that are taken out of secure office environments are exposed to threats such as theft, loss and unauthorized access, potentially becoming weak links in an organization's security chain. What can organizations do to lessen such risks?

Device Tracking and Management

One of the fundamental aspects of device security is the ability to track and manage devices remotely in the event a device is lost or stolen. Three measures that can be taken are:

Location Tracking: Modern device management software includes location tracking features that allow IT departments to monitor the whereabouts of corporate devices in real time. In cases where a device is reported lost or stolen, IT can pinpoint its location, aiding recovery efforts.

Remote Wipe Capabilities: Perhaps more critical than tracking is the ability to remotely wipe data from lost or stolen devices. This function ensures that sensitive information does not fall into the wrong hands, even if the physical device cannot be recovered. Remote wipe capabilities can be triggered automatically based on certain criteria, such as a number of failed login attempts, or can be activated manually by IT administrators.

Data Encryption: To further protect data, devices should be equipped with strong encryption. This security measure ensures that even if a device is accessed without authorization, the information stored on it remains protected and unreadable without the proper decryption key.[3]

Physical Locks and Secure Storage

While software solutions play a primary role in device security, physical measures are equally important to prevent theft and unauthorized access, and may include:

Cable Locks: For devices that are used in semi-public spaces, such as laptops in libraries or offices, cable locks provide a simple yet effective security solution. These locks tether devices to a stationary object, making it difficult for them to be physically removed from the premises.

Secure Cabinets: In environments where devices need to be stored when not in use, such as in schools or shared office spaces, secure cabinets offer a safe storage solution. These cabinets are typically lockable and sometimes also provide charging capabilities, allowing devices to be securely stored and ready for use when needed.

Biometric Security: Incorporating biometric security features such as fingerprint scanners or facial recognition on devices adds an additional layer of security. This technology ensures that only authorized users can unlock and access the device, providing a strong deterrent against unauthorized use.[4]

Regular Software Updates and Audits

Devices should regularly receive updates for security software, operating systems and applications. These updates often contain patches for vulnerabilities that could be exploited by attackers. Additionally, regular audits of security practices and device compliance can help identify potential security gaps before they are exploited. These audits should reveal how devices are used, stored and managed, and whether all organizational security policies are being followed.[5]

Secure Workspaces

Secure workspaces can protect sensitive information and ensure that employees are working in a safe and controlled environment. This involves strategic design and the implementation of security measures to safeguard areas where sensitive work occurs from unauthorized access and other security threats.

The Importance of Physical Layout

The physical layout of a workspace can significantly influence its security. The design should facilitate surveillance and control, making it difficult for unauthorized individuals to access restricted areas without being noticed. Limiting entry points to the workspace can help control access. Each entry point should be monitored and equipped with security measures, such as electronic access control systems to ensure that only authorized personnel can enter.

The layout should maximize natural surveillance. Open areas that are easily visible from multiple viewpoints can deter unauthorized activities. Strategic placement of mirrors and the elimination of blind spots enhance the effectiveness of surveillance cameras and security personnel.

Visitor Management Systems

Measures to manage visitors to a secure building include visitor logging and badging. Badges clearly identify individuals as visitors. These badges can include time limits and specific access permissions.

Visitors should check in at a security desk and be escorted by authorized personnel at all times. This procedure ensures that visitors are monitored and prevented from wandering into restricted areas.

Designated Secure Zones

Designated secure zones are designed to prevent any unauthorized access or eavesdropping. Access to these zones should be controlled through personnel identification tools such as biometric scanners and security codes that change regularly. Once inside a secure zone, further measures such as soundproofing can prevent eavesdropping, and security cameras can monitor for any unusual activity. Communication devices in these areas may also be equipped with encryption technologies to protect data transmission.

Integrated Security Technologies

Integrating advanced security technologies can enhance the security of physical workspaces. These technologies include, but are not limited to, surveillance systems, intrusion detection systems and advanced access control mechanisms.

> **Surveillance Systems**: CCTV systems equipped with motion detection can monitor and record all activities within and around the workspace. Modern surveillance systems can be integrated with digital security measures to provide real-time alerts to security personnel.

> **Advanced Access Controls**: Electronic access control systems that use RFID, biometrics or magnetic stripe cards can ensure that only authorized personnel can enter specific areas. These systems can be

configured to provide detailed logs of who accessed which areas and when, offering an audit trail that can be invaluable in the event of a security breach.

Intrusion Detection Systems: These systems provide an additional layer of security by detecting unauthorized access attempts or movements within secure areas and triggering alarms or lockdowns.

Employee Training and Security Protocols

Employees must be trained on the importance of workspace security and their role in maintaining it. Regular training sessions can help reinforce security protocols and make employees aware of how to respond in the event of a security breach. These sessions should focus on security awareness, meaning that employees should understand the security measures in place and their responsibilities, and be aware of their environment and pick up on and report suspicious activities.

Clear procedures should be established and regularly rehearsed for various security scenarios, including intrusions, fires or other emergencies. Employees should know how to evacuate safely, how to protect sensitive information quickly, and whom to contact in different types of emergencies.[6]

Integrating Physical and Digital Security

The distinction between physical and digital threats is becoming increasingly blurred. Sophisticated attackers exploit vulnerabilities in physical security to breach digital systems, and vice versa. Integrating physical and digital security measures protects both tangible assets and digital data.

Unified Security Protocols

Effective security integration involves unifying security protocols that synchronize physical and digital security operations. By implementing platforms that consolidate management of all security measures, organizations can achieve a holistic view of their security landscape.

Centralized security management systems comprise one such platform, which integrates surveillance systems, access controls, cybersecurity solutions and incident response mechanisms. By centralizing the management of these diverse systems, organizations can monitor all security facets from a single point, enhancing the ability to detect and respond to incidents more quickly and effectively.

Integration allows for real-time data sharing between physical and digital security systems. For instance, an unauthorized access attempt detected by a physical access control system can instantly alert digital security teams to monitor for potential cyber intrusions linked to the same event, thereby facilitating rapid containment and mitigation.

Coordinated Incident Response

A truly integrated security strategy extends beyond just monitoring and includes coordinated responses to incidents that encompass both physical and digital realms. As such, cross-domain incident response plans need to be in place. When an incident occurs, it's crucial that the response is unified across both physical and digital teams. For example, a security breach in a data center might require physical security personnel to secure the site and digital security teams to assess and mitigate any data loss or system compromise.

Additionally, regular training exercises, called simulated cross-training exercises, involving both physical security and IT teams can prepare staff for joint response scenarios. These exercises should simulate real-world incidents that require both physical and digital responses, helping teams understand their roles and how they interconnect during an incident.

Continuous Improvement and Adaptation

The security environment is dynamic, with new threats constantly emerging. An integrated security system must not only be robust but agile, and capable of evolving with the changing threat landscape. Continuous improvement must be a core aspect of integrated security strategies and is achieved through regular reviews and updates of security protocols, systems and technologies to incorporate advancements in security methodologies.

Agility also requires feedback loops and incident analysis. Integrating feedback mechanisms into security operations can significantly enhance adaptive capacities. Analyzing incidents thoroughly to understand what went wrong and what worked can provide invaluable insights that drive the continuous refinement of security strategies.[7]

Safeguarding Financial Data through Comprehensive Security

Financial institutions for obvious reasons are at high risk of cyberattacks. The primary concern of course is the security of financial data. A large financial institution we will use as our example has extensive operations and a network of data centers spread across the globe, and it faced an increasing array of threats to its systems. Recognizing the critical need to protect sensitive financial data, the institution embarked on a strategic overhaul of its security measures to create a fortified barrier against both physical and digital threats.[8]

The institution operated numerous data centers and consequently processed millions of transactions daily, and hence stored vast amounts of sensitive data. When the institution conducted security risk assessments in its digital and physical realms, significant vulnerabilities in the institution's security protocols were discovered, even though the institution had taken steps to solve these vulnerabilities.

The primary challenge was the dual nature of threats faced by the institution. Cyber attackers had increasingly sophisticated tools at their disposal, capable of bypassing traditional digital defenses. Simultaneously, physical breaches had shown that tangible access to systems could provide backdoors into the digital realm. The isolated approach to handling digital and physical security in silos was no longer viable, necessitating a unified strategy to safeguard against integrated threats. Recognizing the intertwined nature of physical and digital security, the institution embarked on a holistic upgrade of its security protocols, including the following:

Holistic Security Upgrades: The institution overhauled its existing protocols to fully integrate digital and physical security measures. This integration was facilitated through the implementation of unified control systems that monitored access to data centers and network activity simultaneously, ensuring that any anomaly, whether physical or digital, triggered a coordinated response.

Advanced Threat Detection Systems: The deployment of AI-driven surveillance systems revolutionized the institution's monitoring capabilities. These systems were equipped with algorithms designed to detect unusual behavior patterns within the network and at physical access points. Alongside these, the institution enhanced its cyber defenses with network threat detection software that analyzed data flow for potential cybersecurity breaches, providing a comprehensive surveillance blanket over the institution's operations.

The integration of these advanced security measures was put to the test when a coordinated attack targeted several of the institution's data centers.

The attack was sophisticated, involving simultaneous attempts to physically access data centers and to breach network security. The institution was able to safeguard its assets through its integrated response:

Coordinated Detection and Response: The unified security system proved its efficacy almost immediately. The AI-driven surveillance alerted security teams to unusual physical access patterns at the same time that network monitoring software 263 identified suspicious data movements. This simultaneous detection enabled a swift, coordinated response that prevented the attackers from penetrating sensitive areas.

Prevention of Data Compromise: Quick action by the security teams, guided by integrated protocols, ensured that the attackers were unable to access or extract any sensitive financial data. The physical intruders were apprehended, and digital access attempts were blocked, safeguarding crucial financial information.

The incident provided valuable insights into the strengths and potential areas for improvement in the institution's security strategy.

Effectiveness of Integrated Security Measures: The incident underscored the effectiveness of integrating physical and digital security systems. The coordinated approach allowed for rapid identification and mitigation of threats, demonstrating that unified systems are crucial in the modern security landscape.

Need for Ongoing Adjustments: The dynamic nature of security threats, especially in the financial sector, requires continual evolution and adjustment of security measures. The institution recognized the need to regularly update its systems and protocols to respond to emerging threats and to incorporate new security technologies as they become available.

The experience of this financial institution highlights the importance of comprehensive security strategies in safeguarding financial data. By integrating digital and physical security measures into a unified framework, the institution not only thwarted a potentially devastating attack but also set a new standard for security within the financial industry. This proactive approach to security, leveraging advanced technologies and continuous improvement, is essential for any organization aiming to protect its data from the sophisticated threats of the 21st century.

Endnotes

1 "What Is Data Center Security?", Cisco, https://www.cisco.com/c/en/us/solutions/security/ secure-data-center-solution/what-is-data-center-security.html; "What Is Data Center Security? Why Is It Important?," Fortinet, https://www.fortinet.com/resources/cyberglossary/data-center-security.

2 "Back-up and Redundancy: What's the Difference?", Capture Blog, https://www.capture.co.uk/ resources/backup-redundancy-differences-data-recovery/ Redundancy in Systems: The Key to Reliability, Availability, and Performance (systemsatscale.io), https://systemsatscale.io/basics/ systems/redundancy/.

3 "What Is Mobile Device Management (MDM)?", https://www.samsara.com/guides/mdm/.

4 "What Is Physical Security? How to Keep Your Facilities and Devices Safe from On-site Attackers," CSO Online, https://www.csoonline.com/article/566635/what-is-physical-security-how-tokeep-your-facilities-and-devices-safe-from-on-site-attackers.html; "Twelve Best Practices for Physically Securing Laptops and Other IT Devices," https://www.real-timenetworks.com/ blog/12-best-practices-for-physically-securing-laptops-and-other-devices.

5 "The Importance of Regular Security Audits," https://www.datasecurity-integrations. com/ types/ importance-regular-security-audits/.

6 "Training Employees to Follow Security Protocols," Fixinc, https://www.fixinc.io/resources/ train-employees-security-protocols.

7 "Adaptability and Continuous Improvement: The Agile and Lean Path to Sustained Success," https:// agility-atscale.com/principles/continuous-improvement/.

8 "Safeguarding Financial Data: The Importance of Data Protection," Outseer, https://www.outseer.com/ fraud-protection/safeguarding-financial-data-the-importance-of-data-protection/ FTC Strengthens Security Safeguards for Consumer Financial Information, available at https://www.ftc.gov/news-events/news/ press-releases/2021/10/ftcstrengthens-security-safeguards-consumer-financial-information-followingwidespread-data.

CHAPTER 15

MEASURING AND ENHANCING YOUR CYBER QUOTIENT

This book has provided a step-by-step approach to strengthening an organization's cyber defenses. The culmination of the tactics and tools is the Cyber Quotient (CQ), which is a comprehensive metric that assesses an organization's readiness and resilience to defend against cyber threats. This chapter explains what the CQ is and how it works, and how an organization can become better equipped to handle the dynamic nature of cyber threats.

Deploying the Cyber Quotient

The Cyber Quotient is a multifaceted metric that evaluates your overall cyber resilience by incorporating four key components:

Cyber Consciousness: At the organizational level, awareness of vulnerabilities and exposure to cyber threats.

Cyber Preparedness: The organization's state of readiness to tackle cyber challenges as they arise.

Cyber Literacy: Educating the workforce on cybersecurity terminology and concepts.

Cyber Response: The organization's capability domestically and abroad to shut down cyberattacks.

How to Improve Cyber Consciousness

Cyber consciousness involves being aware of potential vulnerabilities and exposure points within the organization's digital environment. To improve Cyber Consciousness capability:

Conduct Regular Assessments: Regularly audit your systems to identify potential vulnerabilities. Use vulnerability scanning tools and penetration testing to uncover weak points.

Stay Informed: Keep abreast of the latest cyber threats and trends. Subscribe to cybersecurity news, participate in industry forums and attend conferences.

Promote a Culture of Awareness: Encourage all employees to be vigilant about potential cyber threats. Regular training sessions and awareness campaigns can help foster a security-conscious culture.

How to Improve Cyber Preparedness

Cyber Preparedness is based on awareness plus strategic planning. To improve Cyber Preparedness capability:

Get Ready for the Unexpected: Preparedness involves having the right plans and measures in place to handle cyber incidents effectively.

Develop an Incident Response Plan: Create a detailed incident response plan that outlines specific actions to take during a cyber incident. Ensure all employees are familiar with this plan.

Perform Regular Drills: Conduct regular drills and simulations to test your incident response plan. These exercises can help identify weaknesses and areas for improvement.

Invest in Redundancy and Backup Solutions: Ensure that critical data is backed up regularly and that redundant systems are in place to maintain operations during an incident.

How to Improve Cyber Literacy

Cyber literacy is no longer the focus of the technology function in your organization. As this book has stressed, people are a vulnerable point of attack by cyber criminals. To improve Cyber Literacy capability:

Get a Handle on the Language of Cybersecurity: Cyber literacy involves having a solid understanding of the terminology, concepts and technologies related to cybersecurity;

Provide Training and Education: Offer ongoing training programs for employees at all levels. Focus on common threats, security best practice, and the use of cybersecurity tools;

Simplify Complex Concepts: Break down complex cybersecurity concepts into understandable terms for non-technical staff. Use analogies and real-world examples to illustrate key points; and

Encourage Continuous Learning: Promote a culture of continuous learning. Encourage employees to pursue certifications and attend workshops to stay updated on the latest developments.

How to Improve Cyber Response

Cyber response capability requires an all-hands approach through training and education, and the deployment of effective technologies. To improve Cyber response capability:

Establish Clear Protocols: Define clear protocols for responding to different types of cyber incidents. Ensure that roles and responsibilities are well understood.

Leverage Advanced Technologies: Use advanced threat detection and response technologies to identify and mitigate threats in real time. Artificial intelligence and machine learning can enhance your response capabilities.

Foster Collaboration: Collaborate with external partners, such as cybersecurity firms and law-enforcement agencies, to enhance your response efforts. Sharing information and resources can improve overall resilience.

To Be Resilient Means to Be Vigilant and Prepared

Enhancing your Cyber Quotient is an ongoing process that requires continuous effort and commitment. By focusing on cyber consciousness, preparedness, literacy and response, you can significantly improve your organization's resilience against cyber threats. This approach will protect your digital assets and will ensure the trust your organization has built with customers, suppliers and stakeholders will be sustained in the event of a cyber incident.

The introduction to this book cited some alarming statistics. You don't have to be one of them.

Conclusion

Navigating the Digital Frontier with Cyber Certainty

I would like to close the book with a few remarks to emphasize certain points.

Cybersecurity is not merely a technical endeavor but a holistic approach that comprises technology, processes and, most importantly, people. The approach requires an understanding of the principles of digital security; the role of artificial intelligence and cloud security in digital security; and the practices that fortify an organization's digital defenses. Be reminded that new challenges will always emerge. You can protect your business through continuous learning, awareness, and agility, and leading your organization by emphasizing the collective responsibility that everyone must contribute to including:

Adaptability and Continuous Learning: The digital landscape is akin to shifting sands—constantly changing and evolving. This dynamic nature of digital technology and cyber threats demands adaptability and a commitment to continuous learning. The tools and strategies that are effective today may not suffice tomorrow. Therefore, organizations must remain agile, continually updating their knowledge and tactics in response to new information and emerging threats.

Fostering a Culture of Cyber Resilience: A consistent theme throughout this handbook is the importance of fostering a culture of cyber resilience. Cybersecurity is not the sole responsibility of cyber experts; it requires a collective effort. This involves educating and training employees at all levels, establishing clear policies and procedures, and fostering an environment where cybersecurity is regarded as a fundamental aspect of every role. Such a cultural shift can significantly enhance an organization's capability to prevent, respond to and recover from cyber incidents.[1]

The Role of Business Leaders in Cybersecurity: An organization's leaders must take the lead in nurturing a cyber secure culture, where security is woven into the very fabric of organizational operations. In this endeavor, knowledge is power. Stay updated, stay vigilant, and most importantly, stay collaborative.[2]

Looking Ahead: The Future of Cybersecurity

As we look to the future, the integration of technologies such as AI and machine learning into cybersecurity frameworks presents both challenges and opportunities. These technologies offer the potential to detect and respond to threats with unprecedented speed and accuracy. However, they also require new types of expertise and create novel vulnerabilities. Preparing for these challenges is crucial for sustaining cybersecurity efforts.[3]

As you navigate the digital frontier, remember that confidence in cybersecurity stems from preparedness, knowledge and adaptability. Should you have questions or wish to deepen your understanding of cybersecurity measures, my team at CYPFER is ready to assist and guide you with cybersecurity practices to fit your requirements.

Endnotes

1 "Cyber Resilience for Strengthening Your Organization," https://www.eccu.edu/blog/ cybersecurity/what-is-cyberresilience-why-it-matters-and-how-to-improve-it/ How business leaders can champion a culture of cyber resilience, TechRadar, https://www.techradar.com/ news/ how-business-leaders-canchampion-a-culture-of-cyber-resilience.

2 "Cybersecurity Starts in the C-Suite: Why Every Role Matters," Business Chief North America, https://businesschief.com/leadership-andstrategy/cybersecurity-what-all-c-suite-roles-should-know.

3 "The Future of Cybersecurity: What Will it Look Like in 2031?", https://ecurityintelligence. Com/articles/future-of-cybersecurity-2031/"7 trends that could shape the future of cybersecurity in 2030," World Economic Forum, https://www.weforum.org/agenda/2023/03/trends-for-future-of-cybersecurity/.

About the Author

Daniel Tobok is a seasoned expert in the field of cybersecurity, with nearly two decades of experience at the forefront of digital security and intelligence.

As the CEO of CYPFER, Daniel has led the company to become one of the fastest growing businesses in the cyber security sector by developing a blueprint for businesses to think, prepare and respond preemptively to digital threats, thereby avoiding commercial disruption and securing digital assets.

His journey in the cybersecurity landscape began after attending York University in 2005, when he founded Digital Wyzdom. This first venture was later sold to TELUS, where Daniel continued to shape their Digital Forensics and Security Consulting Division.

He has personally overseen more than ten thousand cyberattack reviews and has been instrumental in numerous successful recovery missions. Apart from his business achievements, Daniel is a highly sought-after speaker and thought leader in the field. His expertise is regularly featured in global media, where he provides insights into current cyber threats and strategies for defense. He is also a recognized authority in courtrooms and among financial firms across North America.

His visionary approach continues to influence the global discourse on cybersecurity, positioning him not only as a leader in the field but also as a pivotal figure in shaping the future of digital security and resilience. Connect with Daniel Tobok @ www.tobok.com.

START YOUR COMPANY ON THE PATH

TO CYBER CERTAINTY

Use the link below to engage Daniel Tobok and CYPFER to create a path to Cyber Certainty for your business.

https://cypfer.com